D1539257

Contents

Dedication

This book is dedicated to…

My parents, Earnie and Peggy Cornelius, who taught me to stay positive, believe it to achieve it, and that anything is possible.

My husband, John, for understanding and supporting my passion.

My daughter, Summer, for lasting love, beautiful creativity, and helping people together as a Mommy Daughter team.

Angels Grace Hospice for opening the door for me to help dying patients and their families through handholding reflexology for symptom management and the power of love through touch.

Jamie Silver, my writing and poetry partner for 10 years, who inspired me through her book about her dear son, Ben. Leslee Serdar for intuitive reality checks. Barbara Keenan Loster for wise insight.

Elaine and her Mom, Ruth Wilkes for sharing their advice as published authors and keeping me motivated to the end. Vicki Dau and Kim Brondyke for being detail oriented, organized life savers. Samantha Dench for showing me by example that a book can be completed while balancing family and work.

Barry Schimmel for inspiring me to create the acronym for Restore Joy which epitomizes my life purpose of spreading joy, love and hope.

Thank you to all my clients, family and friends for believing in me and making this possible!

~Joy Lucinda

Joy's Story

Joy Lucinda has worked as a healthcare professional with hospice, persons with dementia and their families for over 20 years. Since 2010, Joy has taught massage therapists, reflexologists, and health care professionals how to incorporate alternative therapies into every day care for symptom and behavior management in tandem with love and connection through touch.

As she became more aware of her intuition and ability to see people on the other side as a medium, she felt led to focus more on helping people through their grief. Joy has developed simple, easy to apply, life changing strategies and holistic approaches she presents through her *Restore Joy After Loss* programs. These include workshops, coaching, corporate team building, health care trainings and retreats for professionals and laypeople as they grieve.

Introduction

"Grief is the price of love."
~ Glennon Doyle Melton

Wouldn't life be great as an insouciant? A person who is free from worry, concern or anxiety? How long has it been since you laid in the grass and watched the puffy white clouds roll by on a sunny, summer day? Think of this moment. Then think of how light your life felt before loss. Is it possible for that lightness to come back? Yes, it is.

However, grief invades all aspects of our lives like a raging, out of control forest fire. Moving, getting fired, a loved one dies, a pet dies, friends come and go, empty nests, regrets, getting a failing grade, bankruptcy, significant weight gain, miscarriage, postpartum depression, not meeting expectations of our loved ones. All of these things, and many more, are major losses.

Then, on the other hand, there are everyday losses such as our spouse working late, a homemade dinner is burnt, a best friend has to cancel a long-awaited dinner with you, and the list goes on. We even grieve stupid decisions, arguments from the past.

Elisabeth Kubler Ross, one of the pioneers of death and dying research, discusses how we experience "little deaths" every day. In other words, minor everyday losses we experience prepare us to be able to deal with the major ones on some level. However, this preparation doesn't necessarily make healing from the major losses any easier.

Loss creates an emptiness, a longing, a confusion, a daze. Everyday life often takes a back seat to the grief. Have you noticed how heavy the emotions that accompany loss feel?

Here are some questions for you to ponder.
- How would it affect your daily routine if you had a refrigerator in the front seat of your car that completely blocked your view on your right and gave you no elbow room?
- What would it be like to have a 20 pound barbell in your already heavy purse as you walk through the mall?
- Or, imagine hiking with a case of water bottles in your backpack as you climb uphill.

These are just a few examples of what happens as we hang onto emotions after loss. They ride with us and sit on our shoulders. They drag us down or pester us like a persistent mosquito.

Yet we wonder why we're tired as we trudge through each day without the hope of ever moving forward. We blame the loss, but ultimately, it's the rage and anger, grief and sorrow, blame, and guilt, that make for oppressive travel companions. Unfortunately, emotional baggage doesn't have a weight limit.

But there is HOPE!

Remember the 1980's video game *Frogger*? The premise is to move the frog through traffic then across a river on moving logs to get to the next level. After playing *Frogger* for a while, a pattern emerges and getting through traffic is no b ig deal at all. However, there are at least 20 or more splats before going into automatic pilot with the joystick to get to the other side of the road.

The emotions that accompany loss hit us much like the cars in *Frogger*. We feel physical and emotional pain run over us and then struggle to get up again for the next task on our day to day itinerary. But it does get easier over time.

It is possible to get to the point where you can objectively observe the "traffic" in your environment and in your head without any fear of the emotional or physical pain. I will show you how. (See Chapter 4.5 R.E.S.T. to Restore)

The good news for you is that you are HERE reading this book NOW! Together, you and I will apply strategies for you to move forward while balancing everyday responsibilities with grieving.

During a recent meditation, I heard the words "Learning is the fuel, and then we drive." We all go through phases of learning and focus, then move forward with application and implementation. And then, when our tank empties, we learn again.

This book is a learning tool, a guide, to help you move forward after any kind of loss. The exciting part is that you will be able to implement many of the strategies and tools immediately and easily into your life to see what happens. After a while of implementing, there's a point where you won't want to go back to who you were before. Just like restoring an old house, you will tear out the old rotted stuff and redo the foundation while keeping the beauty of the original. Then you add some modern features to make it your new home (Spoiler alert: This will involve building it with peace, love and joy).

But why talk about joy? You may not be able to even imagine joy right now if you've experienced a major loss recently. However, joy and sorrow can co-exist and cross paths simultaneously even while you grieve. David Kessler, a protégé of Elisabeth Kubler Ross and author of *Life Lessons: Two Experts on Death and Dying Teach Us About the Mysteries of Life and Living*, says:

> "...like it or not, change happens, and, like most things in life, doesn't really happen to us – it just happens."

Just that awareness can free you of holding onto blame, guilt and other emotional pains while overthinking why the loss happened. (See Chapter 4 Stop Overthinking)

Awareness is a beautiful peaceful way to "see" where you are emotionally, while still acknowledging the feelings without feeding them with negativity. With awareness, you can look your grief directly in the eye, tell it to "Go to hell!" then gradually it will free itself from invading all your thoughts every day.

Kahlil Gibran, author of the 1923 allegory *The Prophet* writes:

> "Then a woman said, "Speak to us of Joy and Sorrow."
> And he answered: Your joy is your sorrow unmasked.
> And the selfsame well from which your laughter rises

were oftentimes filled with your tears. And how else can it be? The deeper that sorrow carves into your being, the more joy you can contain. Is not the cup that holds your wine the very cup that was burned in the potter's oven?"

You may embrace this concept of co-existence, or you may feel unworthy of joy during grief. For example, you may be feeling guilty about all of things you should have done, or that you should have known better. However, you feeling this way doesn't make the co-existence of joy and sorrow any less true.

*"If you choose to do so,
You can feel peace in a moment of stress,
joy in a time of sadness,
and energy during a time of fatigue."
~ Robin Sharma*

What does it mean to be happy or joyful anyway? Is it content-ment? Is it having no stress? Is it having what we think we want?

When I lived in Prescott, Arizona I would have said I was happy, very happy actually. In hindsight, I wasn't. I found this place in a literal dream and moved there two months later. It was meant to be, right? And, even so, there were happy times sprinkled in between. Driving south on Gail Gardner Way, I was greeted by a huge pine-filled mountain and a moment of awe in my heart. I gazed from the grassy mesa into the full moon beams wondering if she was shining silver or pale yellow. I watched the sunset over the reclining goddesses shaping the mountain range. I smelled the vanilla bark of ponderosa pines and listened to the creek ripple by. I met beauti-ful people at the square, Coffee Roasters, and elsewhere. I spent numerous hours road tripping to visit hospice clients throughout the vast mountainous desert.

But there were also the struggles. My joy was shadowed by stress of broken expectations and general discontent.

However, after I moved away from there, I realized my definition of happiness had been getting what I wanted and expected, then blaming the world because I wasn't.

Happiness was receiving validation to judge my worth. But as I went through trials, embarrassments, and hurts, I finally settled in. Happiness was there all along, of course, not of my doing. It was and is an ever-present state of *Being*.

If you ask what people want out of life, most people would say they want to be happy. But being happy is but a drop in the ocean compared to the state of joy where unconditional love lives. Here grief simply cannot exist.

Interestingly enough, even though I chose to move to Illinois to be with my husband, I grieved leaving Prescott for 7 years, intensely.

Four years after leaving, we went back to Prescott for a family vacation. I was joyous to go, but disheartened when the people I went with didn't have the same connection and passion I did for my "place." I drove to my old apartment, stomping grounds, and hiked some usual places while tears welled right behind my eyes. I felt a despondency overwhelm me every time we were staying at someone's house instead of experiencing my memories. I felt a desperation to fit in as many sites as possible, and each day to fill my grief void in my heart, chest, and gut. I felt dread for the time when we would leave.

Then the day came. I was sad, but okay until we were driving away 70 miles per hour southeast on Highway 69. All the sudden, I felt a huge lump fill up my chest and throat as four-letter words starting with F were spilling out of my mouth and my tears poured out hysterically. I had my hand on the door handle pondering if jumping out and walking back was a better choice than going with my family. I felt like Francesca passing by her soul mate Robert in the last scene of *Bridges of Madison County* with her hand on the door handle to open it to true love or stay true to her husband and children. At that moment, I felt her pain as I didn't jump out of the car and I went with my family "home."

I was numbly aware how for one moment of my grief I felt the complete agony a person considering suicide feels for minutes, hours or days. And it all had to do with regrets, doubting all the choices in my life that led to this, and complete and utter surrender as I felt my perceived freedom and happiness ripped away. It was an illusion. But it was real too. If you are grieving—you understand.

For the next three years, I was still grieving and desperately building my road back to Prescott in any way I could. And I was feeling the cumulative pain from my distant past of all of the people I lost, animals that died on our farm, break ups, getting fired, and, as said many times before, regrets. But, the heavy emotions of self-blame I carried with me day to day were not only hurting me physically, emotionally and mentally, but negatively affecting my personal relationships and my work performance.

Then after years of working in hospice and dementia care with patients and family caregivers, I entered a new phase as a poet, reflexologist and intuitive energy practitioner and medium. I learned how to change my own energy and be aware of my true emotions. To find peace in loss. To find joy in helping others no matter where I live.

This leads us to today, to this book, to going with you as you wonder how to get through your grief journey, let alone feel joy again.

Did my grief heal? Yes, on some level, much like a scar heals. The grief is still there in the place I felt it when I experienced the losses, but without the rawness, the intense pain, and the trauma of how it created the wound.

So, that's why our goal together isn't to obliterate grief. You must let it heal itself as much as it can and cherish its place where it lives in your everyday life from the moment of loss to the present moment. Grief is much like past love letters for old flames. Over time we can read them without remorse or regret and instead with fondness, curiosity and reverence.

In this book, I will illustrate a virtual roadmap of where your happiness resides and how to rid yourself of the heaviness and shadows around your joy.

Getting to joy is possible, even in the midst of suffering, grieving, worrying, being scared, anger and rage and other heavy emotional states. I will show you how as we travel together.

"While the experience that originally caused the hurt

remains unchanged, the way we feel about our suffering
is where we find our power."
~Gregg Braden

There's a reason you picked up this book at this time. You've had just enough pain that you are ready to move forward away from it and leave it behind on some level.

This is not as much a book about how to deal with your grief, but rather how to live everyday while you're grieving and find some joy along the way. This includes honoring the grieving process and what will be learned from it. It's not meant to deny or ignore your grief either. However, everyday life demands doing tasks, interacting with family, going to work and many other obligations.

Also, the information in this book is not to imply the grief of any loss ever goes away. Instead, it's a practical go-to resource guide that will show you how to:

- Release heavy emotions with ten second to three minutes strategies
- Balance your emotional state, stress and tension
- Gauge and adapt your reactions to people and situations around you

As a result, like putting on a new pair of glasses, you'll be able to see where you're at in your grief journey while moving through life easier and with less tension and stress. These strategies also shine the light on your loss in a way that it's like watching a "movie" of what happened.

You'll be able to objectively ask yourself, *What Else Is Possible?* You can start envisioning what it would look like to move forward, while honoring your loss, whether it be the death of a loved one, a divorce, job loss, moving to a new place, or simply entering into a new phase of life.

You'll also be able to react kindly with detachment to the relatives, friends, and coworkers who don't know what to say or do while you grieve. There are simple ways for you to create peace and compassion for them regardless of what they say or do.

It will also enlighten you on what truly brings happiness. It revolves around community and helping others, while honoring yourself.

It's about restoring joy after any kind of loss. There's a strategic approach for those of you who need that, but also you can use your own awareness to pick and choose what strategies resonate with your state of mind and emotional state.

Recently, I was sitting on a blanket under a tree next to the path at a local forest preserve. A family was walking past and their little two-year-old girl in the stroller was holding a trail map. She looked over at me, smiled, pointed to the map and said, "I am here!" Sometimes, we need to objectively see where we are on a map so the journey to joy doesn't seem so elusive and daunting when we only see a part of the path ahead.

Each chapter represents a letter of the acronym RESTORE JOY. The only exception to this is the "R.E.S.T. to Restore" chapter after the Chapter 4. Although there's a flow from chapter to chapter, I encourage you to open the book up to any page when you're dealing with an issue. After all, part of restoring joy is trust that you will get the answers you need when you need them. Different strategies are scattered throughout the book.

At the beginning of each chapter, you'll determine where you are on your map. There's a list of what should be packed and ready to go for that particular leg of the journey.

Each chapter ends with an affirmation, mediation, or quote for you to use whether you're sitting still, doing dishes, or walking the dog. What I will be showing you is easily applied to everyday life and can usually be accomplished in seconds or minutes. You will not have to adopt any type of detailed or deep philosophy or practice. You'll simply be renovating your life one piece at a time with the simple tools.

Just like our trip together, the chapters follow the journey from heavy to light. The first 5 chapters are the most detailed. After all, clearing years of stress, emotional pain and trauma takes some effort and reflection.

Then, subsequently, the road trip to joy gradually eases up and gets lighter. This leg of the trip is going to be like getting your second wind during a run. You'll most likely feel hopeful and energized as you get closer to the destination.

So, are you ready for your peaceful and insightful road trip with and through grief? Great! Get into the 1968 VW van with me. I'm your loyal travel companion to your destination: JOY! We will gradually restore it along the way as we ride together through your landscape of loss, grief and hope.

The beauty of this journey will astound you! Your favorite snacks, maps, and music are ready. The tank is full. Our emotional baggage is packed and in the back. The tires are aired up. Time to en-JOY the ride as we drive together to all the things we've ever wanted on the other side of our fear, anger, disappointment, sorrow, and guilt.

As we take rest stops along the way, we will talk about ways to use ceremonies and practical mindset strategies to honor where we are with each step. Again, easy, simple, and mindful. A way for heart to kindly connect to the hardship. But for now, let's step forth.

Here we go!

Chapter 1:
Release Resistance

"Resistance is futile."
~ The Borg, Star Trek: The Next Generation

I love how one word can say so much. "Futile" means something that won't succeed or is unimportant. An example of futile is someone trying to stop a plane that has already left the ground.

And yet, what do we do when stress, grief, or other heavy emotions kick in? Resist! Resistance leads to being physically and/or emotionally locked up and tense. We often play Tug of War with our feelings and the feelings of family members, friends, and co-workers. The one who lets go of the resistance of the rope stands tall, and simultaneously the one pulling falls down.

The Borg can teach us a lot about the futility of resistance. For those of you who were not nerds in college, The Borg in the 1990's TV show *Star Trek: The Next Generation* were a collective of human androids who listened to all of the same programming and did what they were told. Their sole purpose was to capture and assimilate people into their robot humanoid slave society to create a superhuman intelligence collective. The Borg looked very ominous, like robot zombies dressed in black, flying in their massive black, industrial, super creepy, cubical ship.

The Borg told their captors, "Resistance is futile." In other words, give up now because there's not a chance in hell that the captors will make it out of the cube alive. The ones who resisted were assimilated after a long drawn out fight until they were exhausted and had no choice to relent.

In 2005, I went with my friends to the *Star Trek: The Next Generation* Experience in Las Vegas. I absolutely loved standing on the deck of the Starship Enterprise and pretend flying at warp speed. As we went down one of the hallways of the so-called USS Enterprise Starship, I saw a shadow out of the corner of my eye. I looked over down the hall and saw a Borg was walking.

My heart stopped, and I could hardly breathe. Even though I knew it was a guy dressed as a Borg, my mind raced to what would happen if I was captured by him and being forced to follow orders without question and assimilate (i.e. conform!)—MY WORST FEAR! Because of this, I forced my way to the back of the crowd to protect myself. I didn't sigh until I left the experience. The relief was exhilarating, and I felt so much lighter as I laughed at my silliness.

Gary Zukav, author of *Seat of the Soul*, says that when you resist, and you don't know that you can **shift your attention** to something that's greater than you, then you'll be trapped in the lower levels. Trapped!! This implies inflexibility, lack of freedom, and a whole other level of grief. Doesn't this motivate you to look at where you are resisting life and doing something about it?

So, here's the real deal about stress. Our bodies don't know the difference between a real or a fake Borg, grief, anger, sadness, and working too much. Even the minor stress of spilling a drink on the table, or losing your keys still can result in the same stress response. All the body knows is that it's scared, then it naturally goes into fight or flight mode, and your stress hormones rocket off the charts. This leads to physical and emotional stress, fatigue and your organs not working efficiently.

> *"How we 'feel'—tired or energetic, listless or enthusiastic—*
> *is mental and chemical; it is physiological."*
> ~ Shad Helmstetter,
> *What to Say When You Talk To Yourself*

To go a step deeper about resistance, think of the last time your knee locked up, or your shoulder hurt so much that you could only lift it half way. Do you remember what life experience you were going through when this happened?

Frequently, when I see clients with joint or back issues, I ask them what's going on in their lives. A lot of times my clients will say they're fine and they just twisted something. But, as we continue the session, I learn that a wife is mad at her husband, a woman is taking on too many responsibilities for her family, or the breadwinner of the family just got laid off, for example.

At that point, I gauge the energy around the area that's stuck and guide it to release. This is something you'll learn how to do from this book. Most of the time, my clients with acute or chronic joint or back pain issues will leave my office feeling lighter and with less or no pain. They consider it a miracle. They had no idea or awareness that they were emotionally resisting a solution for whatever was going on in their lives.

Heavy emotions gone unchecked tend to fester then go into the body. The body takes on the emotional energy without judgment, which ultimately leads to pain, inflammation and discomfort. Otherwise, we would spiral into a tornado of emotional turmoil and mental instability.

However, the body naturally wants to eliminate the emotions much like it wants to urinate and defecate to get the waste products out of the physical body. But, how can it do that if you resist change and the emotions get stuck?

The Truth About Stuck Emotions
- Emotions get stored in our energy fields and body organs where they can remain for years waiting for us to have the courage to express them
- Unprocessed emotions of anger, grief, sadness and shame can be a major health threat
- You must process your emotions by learning what they signify and release them
- There's no need to fear emotions that come up. You were designed biologically to feel and release emotions regularly and easily

Therefore, we must learn to gauge what emotions are heavy and how they can be replaced with emotions that are light. Moving out the heavy resistance is critical to our physical and mental health.

Exercise 1

How to Scan the Body for Resistance, Pain and Tension

- Sit or lay with your eyes closed
- Imagine the red straight-line light of an MRI scan starting at your head and slowly going down your body
- Acknowledge where it gets stuck and where there is resistance
- Go further down. Then allow it to pass through with light force to continue the scanning process
- After you scan down to the bottom of your feet, be aware of the areas that were resistant to the scan
- Acknowledge where the scanner got "stuck" or felt heavy

Then ask yourself:
- Is this a physical issue or not?
- Is this resistance mine or someone else's?
- What's the best way to remove this resistance?

Therefore, when you're in a state of real or perceived suffering or angst, ask yourself one or all of the following questions.
- "Am I feeling heavy or light?"
- "Is this emotional state in my highest good?"
- "What will it take to transcend the [your heavy emotion label here]?"

It's important to just ask the question and then "listen to" (feel) that inner voice in the upper chest, stomach, or your heart. Not your mind.

In other words, does it feel heavy (resistant, dense) or light (airy, free, open)? When the upper chest, stomach or heart feels open, that's a "Yes, this is in my highest good." When any of those parts of the body feel closed, it's a "No, this is not in my highest good."

The following table illustrates a scale of your States of Being and states of emotion:

States of Being	Way of Being
God	Omnipotent
Peace	Blessedness
Joy	Delight
Love	Appreciation
Reason	Understanding
Accceptance	Forgiveness
Willingness	Hopeful
Neutrality	Trust
Courage	Empowerment
States of Emotion	**Emotional Response**
Pride	Self-importance
Anger	Aggression
Fear	Anxiety
Grief	Regret
Apathy	Hopelessness
Guilt	Blame
Shame	Misery

Based on the Map of Consciousness by David R. Hawkins, this chart is a great tool to begin your transformative journey. For example, instead of just saying "I feel guilty," or "I feel scared," by referring to the table above you can see where you are in your emotional healing process. In doing this, you can begin to catch glimpse of hope that you are moving forward more than you realized. At the very least, you can objectively acknowledge your current emotional state, so you can set yourself in motion to become lighter.

This is not a continual upward journey. It vacillates. Sometimes you'll fall back down into the depths of blame or guilt and be neutral in the same hour. But, you know where you are — like the girl in the forest preserve saying, "I am here."

According to my own interpretation from working with hundreds of people, typically the levels coincide with different parts of our bodies and energy fields.

Just like going up the scale from bottom to top, if you go up the body from the bottom groin area all the way up to the head, you can deduce which part of the body may be holding onto the level of emotion. This can give you a reference point to look inside yourself to determine objectively how your physical heaviness or symptoms relates to a stuck emotional state.

For example, if you consider where the chakras are located, the lowest base emotions of Shame and Guilt would relate to the groin, bladder, or uterus/prostate near the root chakra. Anger would be near the stomach. Acceptance and forgiveness near the heart, and Peace and Enlightenment above the head.

Energetically, the groin area relates to our need for safety, security, and basic needs for survival like food and water, and a mental need for trust, acceptance, and comfort. Let's say someone is feeling shame or blame based on sexual abuse or other reasons, the person often times has issues with their bladder or uterus/prostate when the respective emotions relating to mistrust or insecurity is experienced and have not been resolved.

Think back to the scan in Exercise 1. Wherever the scan was stuck, look on the chart regarding what emotional state could be affecting that part of the body.

As you go up the scale, the levels become lighter. However, if you have heaviness in any of the levels of consciousness from courage on up, ask yourself: "What needs to be released so I can be free of pain, tension, or rigidity?"

Immediately "listen" to your upper chest, heart, or gut instead of your head. Your body and soul knows the true answer. Alternatively, your head deducts answers only based on logic and thinking. This is a far inferior way to live or solve issues.

Let's say that you're having regrets of your loss. Regrets feel heavy because we feel bad that we didn't make better decisions. But, the positive side of regret, which is at the grief level, is that you're not feeling a heavier emotional state such as guilt, shame or despair.

If you're angry, at least you're not feeling regret or anxiety, but are instead motivated and fired up enough to think about change as a possibility. You're close to courage. You are less stuck than you were at the lower emotional levels.

I encourage you to use the table as a tool for hope and possibility. It's also a tool for self-forgiveness when you fall back into lower states of emotions. At least you can objectively see where you are, then where you can go to move ahead.

This table takes the "figuring it out" aspect away from your healing process because you see a tangible, logical scale of what's happening. Just like the girl in the forest preserve, you can look at it like a map and simply say "I am here." Then you can envision that love, peace, and joy is possible eventually. It's on the table too after all.

To clarify, *states of emotion* are things like guilt, apathy, anger, or fear. They are the emotions in the States of Being Chart from the bottom to Pride. In this state of mind, you're concerned and possibly immersed in your emotional pain and how, if ever, you will get through it. This is the point where you might feel tired, withdrawn, misunderstood, anxious, and regretful.

Throughout this book, I may refer to the *states of emotion* as "lower vibration" or "heavy emotions" or "heaviness." This is not meant to judge feelings and where you are in the process. It's simply a way to differentiate this concept from *States of Being*.

> *"Deeply stored emotions don't go away simply because you have named them and cried a few times, shouted at someone, or talked to a therapist. True transformation*

involves changing our thoughts AND the emotional
connections that keep us stuck."
--Dr. Christiane Northrup

On the other hand, the *States of Being,* which encompass the top half of the Map of Consciousness, are qualities of Love, Joy, Peace, and Enlightenment. The emotions around the States of Being might include trust, forgiveness, optimism, reverence, and serenity. These are the states that you are probably striving for and working toward at various points of your life, especially after loss. Throughout the book, I will be referring to the States of Being also as "higher vibration" or as "light" or "lightness."

This process involves pure unadulterated TRUST. You quiet your mind and turn off your brain to truly feel and perceive what your heart, gut feeling, and soul are saying. Being mindful is the essence of just being here now.

My 87 year old friend, Helen, gave me a beautiful insight on how to be in the moment. She said that she looked in the mirror and observed her face with curiosity and awareness. Then she stepped away. After 10 seconds, she came back to the mirror again to a new reflection, observed, then stepped away again.

Looking in the mirror represents acknowledging the truth of how you look and feel physically and emotionally without judgment in each moment. Alternatively, stepping away from the mirror is akin to illusion, denial and living in Ego. This means that your thinking mind and the people and distractions around you are influencing and shaping your reality.

You might be wondering how it's possible to quiet your mind when there's so much to think about. It's actually pretty simple. Right now, think about and notice all of your current thoughts and the voice that says them. Acknowledge how thinking feels.

Then do this exercise.

Exercise 2

Being in the Moment to Feel Lighter

- Set a timer
- Only look at your hands for 1 minute.
- You can move your hands or keep them still
- When the time is up, acknowledge how your body and mind felt just looking at your hands

What feelings arose? Did you feel antsy or calm? Something in between? Were you judging your hands, or thinking about what you do with them? Did the 1 minute time frame feel short or long? Did you notice anything about your hands you've never noticed before?

When you focus on one object or sensation, even though your brain is thinking, your mind feels lighter in a mindful state. During mindfulness, our brain is not actively figuring out what the thoughts mean nor making them logical. The thoughts are rolling around like a pinball, but the mind is just looking at what you're observing and allowing it to just roll through like a thunderstorm.

To reinforce the feeling of mindfulness, pay attention to one thing at a time. This is how you can start to change your reality and your mindset. You can do it. Anyone can do it!

Rest Stop

- Think of the tedious tasks you do every day or on a regular basis. What are you thinking about when you are

doing them?
- Being mindful is being present with the current activity. Thich Nhat Hanh, author and Buddhist Monk, says, "Wash the dishes to wash the dishes"
- In other words, just do what you're doing now instead of thinking of the future and the past

This is the beginning of you taking charge of how you think and how you feel. Eventually, you'll be able to see your thoughts and feelings as an outsider and be able to shift them. There are strategies for doing this is in Chapter 4 Stop Overthinking. For now, be content knowing the difference between the craziness of our thinking mind and that you're capable of controlling it instead of letting it control you.

In order to have a peaceful mind, hold regular grief sessions to cry or let out anger and rage. My friend, Leslee Serdar, who is an Intuitive Business Coach and Healer, holds her own personal crying sessions on a regular basis to release emotional pain and stress.

Similar to crying, detoxing and nurturing your body by eating healthy foods, drinking plenty water or taking Epsom salt baths or footbaths helps the body release toxins. Simultaneously, stress and tensions go down the drain too.

Conversely, drinking, smoking or eating too much can drive our heavy emotions deeper. It's important to experience your feelings rather than holding them in where they can fester and smolder. Heavy emotions are not necessarily "negative" because they have a function and a lesson that will help you grow in the long run.

Most importantly, joy is possible now even in the midst of grief and other heavy emotions. Stop waiting to lose weight, get a promotion or whatever else you think will make you happy. Be happy now.

Rest stop

The 4 Handy Rules of Thumb

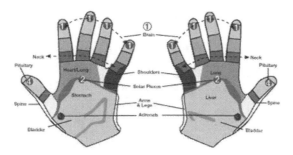

The hands are a map of our whole body.By gently touching the 4 points above on your own hands, you can calm heavy emotions and release body tension.

When we experience physical pain, once it gets bad enough, we finally search out help. Many times, we've tried over the counter remedies, massages, chiropractic, reiki and other fixes that may help for a while. But, even after surgery, many people still have residual symptoms. Here's why:

- Most physical pain is caused from some kind of emotional pain that leads to stiffness, pain, discomfort and resistance in the physical body
- Fixing the physical body first is like filling potholes with gravel and then wondering why they are a hole again after a short time
- Heavy emotions such as anger, guilt, resentment, blame, and unworthiness, literally have weight
- Heavy emotions situate themselves in various parts of the body based on resonance. Anger often settles into the liver, shame often settles into the bladder or uterus, and neglect often settles in the heart.
- Inflexibility in thinking often leads to sore or inflexible joints
- Resisting the release of our heavy emotions is like driving with the emergency brake on

Exercise 3

Emotional and Body Awareness To Decrease Stress

- Allow yourself to be blocked off from your stressful environment or people in your life then feel the resistance in your body and feel it objectively, without emotion
- Ask yourself what heavy situations or emotions you are experiencing or experienced in the past that could be causing resistance
- Say in your head or out loud, "I love and accept myself for who I am" over and over, maybe 1 minute
- Do you feel lighter emotionally? Physically?

This is not a test. This is just to start the ball rolling with you paying attention to your body and emotional tension together to determine which one is influencing the other.

Here's a personal example of my own resistance to change. When my husband and I bought a house, we had a 6 week window where we had no place to live until the new house closed. We were grateful my Mother In Law agreed for us to stay with her. Nevertheless, I was very resistant to staying at her house that long. It wasn't because of her, but because of my fear of being stuck in Illinois forever.

The next day, my left hip was locked up and my leg felt paralyzed and weak. It took me five minutes just to put my pants on because my hip wouldn't move. There was no pain. It was just resistance. It took more than two weeks after we moved in with her for my hip to not lock up when I walked. At that point, I had finally accepted the situation, and I could move on emotionally away from resistance.

Seeing our true selves from the eyes of those close to us can be painful, and, ultimately can cause resistance. Think of times that you felt betrayed or taken aback by a comment that hit an emotional

nerve and revisit how your body felt.
- Did your back tense up?
- Did you cross your arms because you feel rejected (i.e. pro-
tected your heart)?
- Did you feel your body weaken as your Ego deflated?

Good News! When your Ego deflates, you're on the right track! This is the opposite of resistance. It's our spiritual selves saying to let the tension go then rest in a more peaceful way.

When I lived in Thailand, some friends and I went to Bangkok to hang out for a couple of days. It's not uncommon to see stray dogs running around after dark. That night we all walked around a corner and saw a pack waiting with aggressive eyes and on guard stances. We all stood still, tensed up, put our arms up and we started backing up to find somewhere to get away from the wild canines when one of the guys in the group pushed me in front of himself to use me as a human shield. I don't know if my heated reaction to his idiocy and cowardice scared the dogs off or not because I was so pissed off that I could have fought off anyone or any dog. From a primal survival mechanism, I totally get why he did that. However, he should have put a stronger person than me in front of him. Thus, the stupidity.

In the same way, our bodies create tension and take protective measures when it needs to shield us from physical or emotional trauma or pain. When someone is running or lunging at you like the dogs, you would put your arms up like a shield, right? What's the first thing you do when we feel rejected or your feelings are hurt somehow? Similarly, you cross your arms or put them over our belly to protect our heart or the emotionally vulnerable belly from harm. Like mentioned earlier, the stress response is the same whether it's a physical or emotional danger. It's simply a hormonal reaction.

As an energy worker, I often talk with clients about protecting ourselves from bad energy. However, in the same way, someone who puts weight on especially around the stomach area is inadvertently adding on a layer of physical protection from the stress created by your lower states of emotion. Most of them who are overweight have had major life traumas such as sexual abuse, an unhealthy marriage, or abusive or neglectful parents, or PTSD. The solution is release the emotional baggage, then the physical body won't feel in danger anymore.

The body doesn't know the difference between emotional and physical stress. But it reacts accordingly anyway. Physiologically, as the cortisol and other stress hormones build up in your body, many of the "healthy" hormones are turned off and our organs go into low power and efficiency mode. It's no wonder you might tend to overeat when going through fear, anxiety, anger, and other heavy emotions. I said "heavy" emotions! Emotions have weight. They weigh us down. That's why the emotional weight has to be dealt with first! Then body pain, extra body weight, or discomfort will usually take care of itself in the physical body.

If you don't protect yourself emotionally, your body will do whatever it can physically to protect itself. If your body did not take in the heavy emotions we experience, eventually we would fall into a major spiral to severe mental illness. The body isn't able to discern or judge what's happening to it and just receives, as does your subconscious mind.

So, when your body receives your heavy emotions, which ultimately leads to ill health, is there a good reason for you to feel guilty, anxious or worried about how we reacted to a hurtful comment, a snide remark, or a hateful statement? If you do hold onto any lower states of emotions, it means you are putting it on yourself to carry your own and other people's heavy emotional baggage everywhere you go. Because the emotional heaviness causes pain, you may overthink why that person did that or conjure up some version of revenge to feel better. The more this happens, the more toxic your physical and emotional body become.

Then, the longer we carry the baggage, the more tense we get, physical pain sets in, and emotional pain festers. Over time, this leads to dis-ease in the body, which can lead to a literal disease, or acute or chronic pain. All of this was self-imposed by you not allowing yourself to let go of what other people did to you or situations that caused your emotional pain. But ultimately, it was just a physiological flush of hormones after a stress stimulus such as a reaction of panic, anger, or need to be right.

I have a client who worked as an engineer for many years, so she tends to be analytical and likes valid proof of concepts we explore in her intuitive sessions. During one session, she said that her right shoulder was hurting her. I told her that it's no wonder it's sore because there are thought forms of suitcases sitting on her right shoulder. At first, she didn't know how to comprehend this until I asked her why she was thinking of baggage. It turns out her sister had left some baggage at her house and it was cluttering up her living room. She was feeling annoyed with her sister. The weight of her emotional baggage was weighing down on your neck and shoulder muscles. Once I used energy work to remove it, she said her shoulder felt better.

We have to be cautious and conscientious of negative emotions attached to negative thoughts. Emotional baggage has no weight limit and the physical, emotional and mental body can only hold so much weight.

Control is another form of resistance. When it comes to controlling others, we are fearful of what the people around us will say or do to hurt our emotional state. Alternatively, taking control of our own lives allows us to acknowledge triggers to emotional and physical stress and then being able to change our response to a higher state of being such as forgiveness and peace. This is the way to freedom and lightness in our lives despite all the negative things going on around us.

My husband recently pointed out that I tell him "You need to do this." Until he made me aware of this, I didn't realize how much I was a manipulator, not so subtly swaying him to what I want from him or who I want him to be. This type of Puppeteer role is not received well by the strong-willed, decisive people in our lives. Although I had good intentions, I realized my bossy pants approach wasn't working so I had to shift to using my Please and Thank You manners. My Ego hates this and digs in its heels. But through intense sheer will, I am learning suck it up to take the kind and patient road of compassion, love and peace. It gets easier over time, even for us stubborn folk.

According to Virginia Satir's Change Model, "…resistance involves when a foreign element threatens the stability of familiar power structures. People resist by denying validity, avoiding the issue, or blaming someone for causing the problem. Unconscious physical responses can include shallow breathing and closed posture. Resistance clogs awareness."

No wonder grief is so hard to deal with. Our thinking and awareness becomes clouded with grief. It's a foreign element that our emotional body feels it has to fight, much like the immune system automatically fights a virus when it first enters the body. When grief slams into our system, it's very much the same stress response as panic, creating utter chaos in our physical, mental and emotional being.

If you've ever seen a movie with a tidal wave inevitably hitting the shore, people stand in shock watching it come. Then, the panic sets in and they all start running away from it pushing people out of the way to maybe survive. However, is running away the answer if the tidal wave is going to hit you anyway? Why not feel the panic, but watch it in awe instead?

Be curious. Acknowledge its inevitability. Find peace in that space before it throws you around and spits you out. Feel it thrash you around once it arrives. Know that this is the only path at this moment. This is antithesis of resistance and the epitome of surrender because, as the Borg say, "Resistance is futile."

Rest Stop

**Before you make rash decisions, take action impulsively,
or say something you'll regret:**

• Do a 3, 2, 1 countdown in your mind or out loud to reset

your mind
- Stand or sit still for 5-10 seconds to assess where you feel heaviness in the body
- Shake it out through your hands or make a loose fist for 10 seconds to release the tension

This is a strategy I demonstrate for health care professionals and front line care staff who consistently take on their patients' emotional baggage. I tell them to stand for 10 seconds in front of the next patient's door before entering and ask themselves the following questions:
- Am I still thinking about the last patient?
- Does my body feel heavy or light?
- Do I feel anxious or stressed?
- Does my body feel tense?

Asking these questions, allows the caregivers to breathe, pause, and assess themselves before caring for the next person.

After this, I demonstrate the act of literally taking the energetic backpack of the previous patient's issues and stress off of their shoulders, one strap at a time, and leaving it at the door. Then when they leave the patient's room, they take their love for that person with them and leave the emotional backpack of that patient at the door.

Are you carrying other people's burdens around with you? Do you really believe that taking on other people's suffering is helping them? It's not! Most importantly, it's causing you to suffer needlessly.

Rest Stop

Do you want to drive around with guilt, anxiety or blame as your travel companions? Instead, choose the light State of Being that it ideal for a long ride.

Affirmation:
*Now is a good time to pull off the road to
rest, pause, and reset.*

Finger Holds – Using Your Hands to Gauge Your Emotions

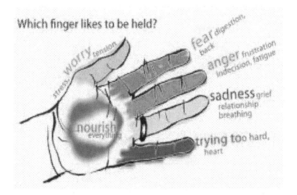

A few years ago, I had a vendor table to educate the staff at the
Alexian Brothers Mental Health Hospital about how reflexology can
benefit mental health symptom management. Instead, the Recre-
ational Therapists educated me about the Finger Holds technique.

When I teach my reflexology seminars, I demonstrate that gently
pulling off on the fingers helps to release tension from the neck up
to the top of the head. One of the emotional benefits is that it also
releases anxiety, agitation, and overthinking. If it's hard to pull off,
this is a sign of resistance, or tension, in the body.

But after experimenting with the fingers holds with more than 50
of my clients, I realized that I had to gauge whether the resistance
in the fingers was an emotional or physical trigger. In doing so, I
found that more often than not the issue was emotional. Once I held
the finger and validated that the client's emotional state mirrored
the emotion represented, the physical issues resolved themselves
once the emotional resistance was released.

This tool is also helpful when a toe or finger is injured, sore, or
inflexible. Use the finger holds as a guide to ask yourself if the
emotion represented coincides with your actual emotional state
related to your stress, family, or job. Once you're aware that's it,

know that you can simply release it through a finger hold. Be kind to yourself. Do the finger hold.

One of my clients spoke with me about the results her recent reflexology session. She said her plantar fasciitis felt much better, but both of her 3rd toes were swollen for 3 days afterward. Since the middle finger and toes are related to anger, I asked if she was mad at someone. It turns out she had a fight with her husband. After 3 days, they had made up and the swelling dissipated.

For depleted caregivers, one of the most common fingers needing help is on the left pinkie. This relates to trying too hard, a negative self-image, and the heart center which leads them to want to care for others. But, in doing so, they often lose their own identity and freedom.

One of my clients who was caring for her Mom who had dementia explained that she woke up every day with nail marks in the middle of her hands. Because she gave so much of her time and energy for the care, the body had to go into automatic pilot to emotionally nourish her while she was sleeping.

I often get asked how long to hold the finger. There's no set time frame, but you'll know when to release the hold when it feels right. A finger hold is like a hug. You hang on until you feel light again, then you let go.

The table below shows which heavy emotions can be released through each finger and the State of Being that remains when you let go.

Finger	State of Emotion	State of Being
Thumb	Worry, Stress, Tension	Peace
Index	Fear	Acceptance/Forgiveness
Middle	Anger, Frustration, indecision, fatigue	Reason/Understanding/ Compassion
Ring	Sadness, grief, relationship, breathing	Joy/ Serenity
Pinkie	Trying too hard/ desperation/broken heart	Love/Reverence

Finger	State of Emotion	State of Being
Middle of Palm	Tension/Low self-esteem	Nourishing and calming self so you can nourish others
Wrist	Harbors heavy emotions like grief, anger, guilt, resentment	Joints are portal to release heavy emotions and tension to create physical, emotional, mental and spiritual lightness

Releasing resistance from your body and mind can be addictive once practiced on a regular basis. Feeling light is the first step for calm and ease to start entering your day. Wouldn't ease be a wonderful gift to embrace? Set a goal of peace and ease when the heavy states of emotions show up at your door.

Let's make this road trip to joy a smooth ride instead of driving with the emergency brake on. And remember, everything you've ever wanted is on the other side of fear. Drive on, dear one.

Chapter 2
Ease Into Neutral

"Rest when you're weary.
Refresh and renew yourself,
your body, your mind, your spirit.
Then get back to work."
~ Ralph Marston

Aung San Suu Kyi is one of the bravest women in our day and age. Born in Rangoon, Myanmar (aka Burma), she studied abroad then came home to take care of her mother, but also to witness the brutal rule of dictator U Ne Win. She initiated a nonviolent movement toward achieving democracy and human rights, which uplifted and fired up the citizens who wanted the dictatorship to end.

From 1989 on she endured 15 years of house arrest for her uprising instead of leaving the country where she could have had freedom. For her brave and persistent efforts to free Burma's citizens, she was awarded the Nobel Prize for Peace in 1991.

The movie *Beyond Rangoon* showed a wonderful portrayal of her as she faced a line of the resistance military force who came to break up the protests. Alone, she stepped ever so gently and slowly toward the line of men with assault rifles pointed at her and ever so gently walked between them and behind them to make a beautiful statement of peace and support for freedom. This was the complete antithesis of the militia rule and the perfect counterpoint to control and ego.

This is an example of the role of Neutrality in our lives. We must step through our problems, fears or heavy emotions, then when we come back to them, we can see the purpose of the resistance. The resistance creates a path you don't want. That's basically it. So, do you mirror the resistance and fight a losing battle? Or, do you stay neutral, balanced, and peaceful to ever so gently move past or through the fear, anger, resentment, and other heavy states of emotions?

As I was researching the concept of neutrality, I had a surprising and very humbling realization. I, Joy, am living in the Neutral phase between Courage and Willingness. I thought for sure that now that I am helping so many people with their grief and in moving forward, I must be moving up the scale. I am--from the Anger and Pride phase to the Neutral phase.

My name is Joy, and people comment on how joyful I am in life and, yet I am ever so far from the ultimate state of Joy. The true realization is how long I had been assuming that *doing* equated to an evolved state of consciousness. In truth though, I am now aware that *being* is the key to opening up to higher States of Being.

Furthermore, neutral is the gear we put our car in when it needs to be towed. It is the gear between reverse (reliving our past) and drive (moving into the future). Essentially, it is "non-doing." It's about letting ourselves be taken to a place to be repaired and reset so we can once again drive ahead toward Joy. So, are you willing to let go of pride to go into neutral and ask for help as you recover balance in your life?

> *"The minute you shift to neutral when you're trying to go*
> *up a hill, you start going backwards."*
> ~ Unknown

Being neutral is a safe zone to rest and recuperation. It's like being stuck in rush hour traffic being at a complete standstill and there's nothing else to do but go with the flow. It's a time to take a breath and sit with what is. See what's around you. Hone in on the sky, the people in the car in front of you, the wildflowers growing in the median, or other things that pass you by driving 70 miles per hour. You may be surprised how little you notice the things you "see" every day.

I remember during a blizzard in 2007 it took me hours to get home from work. However, as I began to creep along, I was driving slow enough to simply watch unique shape of each snowflake land on my windshield. The simple peace of just looking at snow flake gently settle in front of my face took me on a philosophical journey. I was aware of all of the beauty we miss in a pile of snow because we simply move too fast.

Rest Stop

Is your grief landscape passing you by?
Find a rest area to neutralize.

- Walk instead of drive so you can see the beauty as you pass by things more slowly. You can appreciate each step of your journey and notice things you never saw before. Your destination to peace, love and joy is ahead but look here now.
- Is there a flower, a tree, a place to sit and reset?
- Is there a person who is compelled to share their healing gifts with you? Or, give you a smile when you thought no one cared?
- Slow down to let your heart tell you of a place to heal and recuperate.

Maintaining balance and harmony is precarious when obligations and other people create stress. In Chemistry, the ideal pH of water or blood is a neutral 7.0. Below 7.0 is acid and above 7.0 is alkaline. The body works very hard to maintain the blood at neutral despite the state of the body.

So, if you tend to eat a diet of processed foods, sugar, soda, and other acidic type foods, the body goes into stress and survival mode to keep the blood neutral which makes the body work harder constantly to maintain balance. But, if you eat healthy foods such as fruits and vegetables, some nutritious seeds, and other plant based foods, your body is in its happy place. The alkaline foods are able to be metabolized used readily by the body without struggle or stress leading to a balanced state.

This is similar to when we hold onto and buy into the heavy states of emotions. Our emotional being struggles constantly to stay in a neutral state and we tend to fall back in the lower states of emotion such as apathy, regret, and grief. However, when we're in a neutral state or able to surpass neutral, our emotional and spiritual being can just "be" balanced. At neutral, we can catch a glimpse of the horizon where forgiveness, reason, love, joy and peace grow. It's possible and probable now.

You may be wondering what it takes to get and feel balanced. If you go to a chiropractor, physical therapist, or Pilates instructor, the professional checks your body alignment, which is simply evening out the left and right sides of your body. Afterwards, you will literally be more balanced when you walk or do every day physical activities.

But there's an emotional component to this. If the left or right side of the emotional body, including the brain is out of alignment, you will not be balanced emotionally or mentally.

Regarding States of Being chart in the previous Release Resistance chapter, ideally our goal is to keep going up through the levels. However, rebounds are normal especially since grief blows us over and kicks us just when we feel we might be okay.

Conversely, when we're sitting in the level of Neutrality, there is no movement or momentum. This is a time for settling in, doing very little, and un-attaching from ego and the need to do or be what others expect. There is no forcing anymore, only potential power which gets stronger as we evolve into each State of Being.

In the previous chapter, I discussed resistance in the body, especially in the joints and body organs. Regarding emotional balance, there's a different emotional reason for a left knee injury versus right knee injury, for example.

The left side of your body is the feminine side. This is where our heart is. It exhibits positive States of Being such as love, compassion, caring, giving to others, nurturing our children and those who need help and passion for family.

On the flip side, the left side of the body also harbors heavy emotions such as regret, remorse, shame, disappointment, feeling unloved, feeling unworthy, giving too much and trying too hard.

The right side of the body is the masculine side. This is where we exhibit qualities such as strength, ambition, passion for work and accomplishment, courage, and motivation. Conversely, it can harbor heavy emotions such as rage, guilt, grief, rigid control, stubbornness, not wanting to change, and frustration. Do you feel the difference?

Exercise 1

Acknowledge your body and brain

- Is one side more tense than the other?
- Do you notice you have more pain or discomfort on one side versus the other?
- Does one side feel light and airy and the other one heavy and dense?

Just be aware with no judgment. You're just objectively observing your body. Being aware of the difference is the beginning of you taking charge of whether you hold onto heavy emotions or not, and if you truly are ready to feel emotionally balanced again.

The following table illustrates the heavy states of emotions and the light States of Being associated with the two sides of the body. Sometimes it helps to see on paper what our imbalance and misalignment look like so we can do something about it.

	Left Side	Right Side
	Feminine	Masculine
Light	Heart Centered/ Compassion	Task Centered, Objective/ Confidence
Light	Family/Helping others/ Self-Love / Caregiving	Work/Passion/Energy / decisive / moving forward
Heavy	Feeling sad, betrayed, depleted, guilt over family	Harbors Feelings of guilt, grief, resentment, anger, bitterness
Heavy	Trying too hard/ desperation/broken heart	Feeling stuck, unforgiving, apathetic

Exercise 2

How to integrate the left and right sides of your body and brain to be balanced

Cook's Hookup

It's wonderful to feel high on life, but if you're so super-charged that you feel disorganized, scattered or out of control, you'll probably function better if you "get it together." This technique is deeply calming and centering. This feels like a self-hug.

1. Cross left ankle over right
2. Outstretch arms and cross right hand over left
3. Tuck hands under and up and rest them on chest near your heart
4. Breathe calmly and hold for 1 minute

How does it feel to think that you are or might be harboring some of these heavy emotions in your body? How long have they been weighing you down? Does knowing they are there motivate you to shift to the lighter state?

Often, my clients have stiffness, pain, or some kind of organ discomfort primarily on one side of the body. Many of them are literally hobbling into my office because they are literally weighed down from chronic personal and family emotional baggage from the time of childhood to the present. Each part of the body on heavy side that is tense or "asking for help" energetically requires a different process for clearing.

At a senior care professional networking meeting, I met a preacher who offered his spiritual services to seniors in nursing homes. He had a brace on his right wrist and said he fell and fractured it. He also said that his wife had died a few months prior. I explained that it was a good thing that his injury was at his wrist because it meant he was starting to let go of the heavy emotions around grief. Tears welled up in his eyes. I showed him how to simply place his hand on the top of his wrist and feel the arm, shoulder and wrist relax. This is a measure of him being ready, little by little, to release the heaviness while honoring his grief for his wife.

In the last chapter, I mentioned that joints hold onto heavy emotions and become stiff or inflexible. Often, I'll notice that emotional baggage (also known as thought forms) of people in their lives or stressful situations sit between the shoulders and neck. Therefore, we feel the weight of the world is on our shoulders. Once they know the burdens are there, they are aware what needs to be released. Like a ball rolling downhill, the boulder or heavy emotions flow out through the arm, wrist, hand and fingers.

Exercise 3

Releasing Emotional Baggage

Ask someone you know to do this exercise with you. It can be done with one or both sides of the body.

- Gently place your hand over your own wrist or the wrist of someone who is tense and stressed
- Hold it there until the arm, shoulder and hand relax onto the arm of a chair or in the lap
- When this relaxation happens, you can be assured that the heaviness of the emotional baggage is being released
- Look at yourself in the mirror or at the person you helped
- Does one shoulder look higher than another?
- Does that side of the body feel lighter than the other side?
- Repeat on the other wrist

"Rising above barriers or oppositions that dissipate one's energies, the Neutral condition allows for flexibility and a nonjudgmental, realistic appraisal of problems. To be neutral means to be relatively unattached to outcomes. Not getting one's, way is no longer experienced as defeating, frightening, or frustrating."
~ David R. Hawkins, MD, PhD *Transcending the Levels of Consciousness, The Stairway to Enlightenment*

Isn't it interesting how this view of Neutrality is the opposite of resistance, conflict and guilt, which involve control. Instead, at this level you are simply ready to have freedom for self and others and no need to prove anything anymore. You simply live in a nonjudgmental contentment with what is and value calm versus busy-ness.

But, this is not the final destination on your road to Joy. In fact, Neutral is not even an expression of joy, compassion, or love. Instead it's a place to focus on inner healing as you recuperate from despair, depression, grief, fear and guilt. Here, you can look at the past as an education rather than a trauma. You can spiritually start feeling the possibility of love and peace and, in time, are ready to seek the higher States of Being.

But it does take time. And in this time of rest, you can begin to think about what it would take to heal a little bit at a time. When you do have an emotional fallout and feel guilty, scared, or grief emotions again, you can at least be aware of Neutral being your safe place to find the courage to get back to your road to joy.

"It is safe to ask for help."
~ Louise Hay

Rest Stop

Here are some suggestions for inner healing and asking for help while you recuperate:

- Find a friend or family member. Ask them to JUST listen to you. Being seen and heard can help heal.
- Find an elder to talk with to feel loved and safe while receiving their wisdom.
- Intergenerational healing may include drawing, quilting or doing simple interactive activities that won't be focused on talking about grief. Plan these with your kids, sibling or grandparents.
- Buy a stuffed animal to sleep with to bring back nurturing feelings from childhood.

Exercise 4

Strategies to Shift Into Neutral Daily

- If you're in traffic, read license plate numbers or street signs out loud and anxiety won't affect you as much if you're focusing in on meaningless labels
- What's up?
  - » Whether you're sitting or taking a walk, look up, or look in front of you
  - » Often when we walk we're looking down because we're overthinking about our worries or to do lists
  - » The act of looking up turns on your nonjudgmental awareness versus your thoughts
- Receiving - Sit with your palms facing up on your lap or chair arms. Count to 10 in your head. Physiologically and emotionally, this opens you up to receive help and start to heal.
- "Giving up" - Lift your hands above you head with palms up. This sets the intention that you are ready to give your burdens and stress to God or to let it go so you can heal.

Once you reach Neutrality, congratulations! You will have transcended fear, anger and finally had the courage to let go of the past burdens and influences. You will officially be in the States of Being. But don't be discouraged if you're not there yet. Allow yourself to do something for yourself to recuperate and reset.

Chapter 3:
Stop Overthinking

"Overthinking is a special form of fear. This fear becomes worse when adding anticipation, memory, imagination, and emotion together."
~ thepsychmind.com

"Pain changes people, it makes them trust less, overthink more, and shut people out."
~ Unknown

Overthinking can literally make you insane. Here's my story about becoming a raging lunatic. It was not one of my finer moments.

Many years ago, I was obsessed with my boyfriend. He was handsome, an artist, a poet and a great cook. We read books together and enjoyed hanging out in nature. It was love at first sight on my end. Then one night when he didn't show up to the house by midnight, my mind went out of control. I just knew he was cheating on me with his previous coworker. What a jerk! How could he?

By 1 am, I was stomping out of the house to find him at the bar. I saw an ex-con homeless guy I had spoken with in passing at the town square. I had told him my name was Solange. Using an alias was a sane thing to do for safety, right? But as a raging lunatic, I was pouring out my heart and my tears about all the times my boyfriend said "Joy, I love you." The ex-con said, "I thought your name was Solange."

At this point, I was breathless with rage and betrayal, let alone feeling stupid hanging out with a guy at 1 am who just got out of prison. Then, I became even more neurotic because I was thinking, "Oh crap, I'm going to be murdered now." The ex-con, of all people, said to chill and went into the bar to see who was with my boyfriend. He said there was no woman by that description in the bar.

After the good news from the ex-con and my neighbor Jacques who bought me a margarita to calm down. I spoke with my boy-friend the next day. He said he just needed some space. We broke up one month later for good.

There is a happy ending though. The woman I thought he was cheating with is now one of my dearest friends. I met my husband because of her. She met hers because of me. And we still laugh about me being a dumbass that night. To this day, I know that overthinking is a dangerous road to travel.

Everything you're running away from is in your head.
~ Unknown

Most of what's going on in your head is made up scenarios that stress you out for no logical or apparent reason. Overthinking breeds needless worry, anxiety, fear, paranoia and imaginary memories that are recorded in your subconscious mind. When your brain is triggered by similar unreal scenarios later, those imaginary dramas and the emotions attached to them create logic based on something that's not even real! Then the question of what is and what really happened and what didn't becomes blurry.

This is the danger of creating or buying into drama and overthink-ing. Letting your thoughts wander out of control is like digging up an ant hill. Thousands of ants frantically splay out every direction. It's ridiculous and absurd, and yet it is a common human behavior.

This is how your mind works. One thought builds on another, then another until a whole new story of our "reality" is spun out of control. The Truth gets lost in a web of lies or illusion or delusion. The bigger problem is that we start believing the lies as our Truth. For example, saying "I don't know" is more truth than accommo-dating others by saying "I'm fine," or "I'm okay" just to get them off your back.

Our thoughts are much like a rodeo. Sometimes they thrash around like a bucking bronco or a raging bull doing everything to throw us off. Or, they take off running like the barrel racing horses and keep going in circles.

I used to think that if a song was stuck in my head, there was a reason for it, some kind of esoteric meaning. Now, as I learn more about calming the mind, I realize that the song is not something divine as much as my reasoning brain finding memories relating to my emotions stemming from my thoughts. At first, this was disheartening. I asked myself, "Does life have meaning? Was this really a sign from God?" Then, literally, I thought "this song is not stuck; it's looping."". The more you focus on the song the more it loops. This is where switching your mental gears comes into play.

When we think about and focus on a memory, song, or a situation we feel bad about, that's when the emotions step in like emergency responders. There's a recorder in our subconscious brains that keeps a record of our repetitive thoughts. The more we think of drama or despair or gossip or other lower level states of emotion, the more it becomes a habit for our subconscious brains to pull up the overthinking "memories" we set in motion due to worry, stress or anxiety. Fortunately, the opposite is true with memories related to states of being.

Rest Stop

- Have you noticed when you're in a quiet place, your thoughts seem louder and to "talk" lot more?
- Music bypasses the thinking part of the brain and directly affects your mood center.
    » Belt out songs or listen to music to curb your over-thinking mind.
    » Thinking about music does not have the same effect

In the book *The Untethered Soul* by Michael Singer, he writes about the voice in our heads, also known as the annoying roommate. You know that voice. It's the one that keeps talking and talking and commenting on or being skeptical about whatever we're thinking. If this was a real roommate, you would send that person packing. But instead you listen to this insane voice telling you what's right and wrong.

The good news is that this voice is not really you. You are the one that is observing and hearing the voice. You are not the voice. The voice is not looking out for your highest good but is simply reacting to your thoughts.

After reading *The Untethered Soul*, I went through a phase of telling my "annoying roommate" to shut up each time I felt my thoughts go out of control. That did not work at all. My mind kept talking, complaining and judging while my heart and soul were desperately trying to come through.

A strategy I use when my mind is in overthinking mode is to simply say "What else is possible?" to let the sun of truth peek through the clouds. Since I started incorporating this into my routine, the neurotic thoughts do stop each time I ask this question, much like when kids yell "Freeze!" when playing tag. Instead of feeling frustrated, I felt liberated. My mind was simply waiting for instructions based on whatever was in my highest good to change the thought patterns. "What else is possible?" switched gears from worries and scenarios from the past to what possibilities lie in the future.

Rest Stop

- Think of something that worries you or stresses you out.
- How does your brain feel to think about this situation?

Lower level emotions are heavy and clog up your logic because they create resistance.

- Now ask, "What else is possible?"
- How does your brain feel?

Higher States of Being feel light and hopeful because they free your mind of the lower level emotions.

So, to go a step further, when our minds go crazy with overthinking it's like being at a big party with 100 people and loud music. Everyone talks louder, then the whole room gets louder so you must talk even louder still to be heard. And then, what happens to the truth, your authentic thoughts, when this happens in your mind? In addition to other things, the truth gets buried, obstructed, and intermingles with and gets diluted into distracted thinking.

Distraction due to overthinking takes you away from your road to joy much like when you take the wrong exit off the highway. Ultimately, the road trip takes longer, you feel confused and you have figure out where you are so you can get back on track again. Getting off track expends a lot of energy because it shifts you back to lower level emotions. In this case you might say, "Why did I do that?" or "I'm an idiot." Then your brain and the annoying roommate create a bed of commentary about regret and blame.

Staying on course can be challenging because of your everyday responsibilities and obligations as well as dealing with people at work and home. When we are in the midst of grief, chaos and stress, there are many people around us that have good intentions as they offer advice for healing from loss. However, many times their advice or actions are based more from fear and not knowing what to say than something that will make you feel better.

This is all the more reason to make sure that your head is clear as you travel with the heavy emotions surrounding your grief. If you don't, all of the suggestions and well-intentioned solutions will end up clogging up your head and looping around. You may question why you still feel the way you do. Or, you may feel bad that you still cry years later. You might be shrouded with doubt that wasn't there before. Where doubt sets in there is only illusion, a hall of mirrors.

Fortunately, there are simple strategies to overcome these mind dramas before they spiral out of control and lead to regrets.

In Chapter 1 "Releasing Resistance," I mentioned that the body can't differentiate real versus imagined stress. It can't differentiate thoughts from real situations either. So, when you focus on a negative situation, the body awakens the emotional stress response, and chaos ensues in the thinking mind.

Virginia Satir, known as the Mother of Family therapy, created theories about how change impacts organizations. According to Satir Change Model, "chaos leads to loss of belonging which triggers anxiousness and vulnerability. These emotions may set off nervous disorders such as shaking, dizziness, tics, and rashes. Sometimes people will then revert to childhood survival rules. To deal with the chaos, people in this stage need help focusing their feelings, acknowledging their fear, and using support systems. This stage of chaos in vital to the transformation process."

It's important to acknowledge the role of chaos in your thoughts and everyday life. Ideally, this awareness would take place before the waterfall of emotions and physical symptoms flood your body and mind. However, even if it does get to the point where you are anxious or experience things like shakiness or rashes, these signs are a wakeup call reminding you that you can transform yourself to obliterate your thoughts around the chaos even though the chaos is still there.

In high school, my Mom and I loved to watch the game show Jeopardy! After a while it became natural to answer the answers with a question. The same is true when you want to free yourself of irrational overthinking that leads to worry, fear, anger and other states of emotions.

When we try to find reasons for our worries or when we are in distress, that's when the overthinking starts.

However, if we just ask a vague open-ended question and do not answer it, then the subconscious mind will bring forth solutions based on possibilities for your future instead of retrieving every scenario and memory of your worries.

Here are some examples of questions you ask when you are in

distress to counterbalance an out of control mind and to put the brakes on the irrational thoughts. Simply ask them without your mind answering. The first thing that pops into your head is your truth from your soul. If you wait longer than one second to answer, the irrational overthinking mind has set itself into motion.

- What else in possible?
- How does it get it any better than this?
- What would it take to…?
- What is it in me that can change my situation?
- Is this is my highest good to…?

My client "Cristy" has been working for three years at a hospital foundation writing grants while also writing a young adult novel on the side. Even though she's an award-winning journalist, she feels that her supervisors are not utilizing her skill set enough. She feels unappreciated but has to stay at this position for the benefits.

As a result of this, she feels tired when she gets home and procrastinates working on her book by reading novels or thinking about ways to organize her workspace.

According to Zen Habits, "at its root, procrastination is almost always based on some kind of fea…. One of the reasons fear can be so powerful is because it lurks in the dark. So the first step is to shine some light on it – fear hates light." Shining the light on "Cristy's" job and book writing led to her fear of rejection and failure stemming from being raised by parents who didn't validate her accomplishments.

Throughout her session, "Cristy" was talking about how she was rejected by her boss and all of the health reasons and trips that kept her from finishing her book. I asked her "Is this job in your highest good?" She immediately said no. I asked her, "Is writing the book in your highest good?" She immediately said yes. Then I asked her, "What would it take to finish your book?" and she effortlessly listed three ways to get it done by the end of the year, as a smile broke out on her face.

Then regarding her current work situation, I asked, "What is it in you that feels you have to argue with your bosses?" She explained that she feels devalued. I asked her, "What else is possible?" and "Cristy" said she will simply do her job without feeling rejected until she finishes her book.

After she answered these questions, "Cristy" transformed from someone who was scared to move forward and therefore complaining and making excuses to someone who had a clear plan for her own future. At the end of the session, she was smiling and said she felt hopeful. She plans to use these questions to stay on track.

You may wonder why weren't there any "why" questions? When something negative happens, it's common to ask questions like, "Why did this happen to me?" Or, "Why did my sister say that?" First of all, when you ask "what" or "how" questions, usually you receive answers that lead you down only one road. Obviously, if you're traveling down only one road that you know goes to your destination, you can focus on what you must do to get there.

However, when you ask a "why" question another road shows itself. The shape of the letter "Y" illustrates this. Imagine the bottom of the "Y" is the road to your destination, joy. Then you ask a "why" question such as "Why am I doing this?" Immediately, a fork forms in the road, much like the top of the letter "Y."

When you're on a literal trip and you come to a fork in the road, you have to spend some time and energy making a decision which way to go. You might have to reset your GPS or ask for directions because you don't want to delay your trip by getting lost heading the wrong way. But this ultimately takes an unexpected amount of time and creates stress.

At the "Why" fork in the road, one direction is the initial road to Joy. This is the one you were on beforehand that is driven by truth, your highest good, forgiveness, and compassion. This road triggers a love and compassion response. But because you asked why, the other road driven by the mind and ego starts creating doubts, panic and worry about the road to joy. The overthinking mind just took a few steps back to assess the hesitation you had and create crazy irrational reasons to wait. This is what happens when you feel stuck.

How much energy are you expending being stuck all because you have to know why? Does it really matter? Listen to that voice of your soul instead. It will lead you forward and the why's won't matter anymore. You will be able to forgive or see others with compassion instead of taking things personally and buying into drama. Get back on your road to joy, take a breath, and ask, "What else is possible?" Then you will move ahead with ease to the next phase.

Exercise 1

How to take control of your overthinking mind

Download the HEADSPACE APP onto your phone or tablet.
It has 3 to 10-minute meditations that retrain your brain how to let your mind wander then harness your thoughts at will to come back to center.

OR

Imagine a vacuum hose sucking out the thoughts in your head. The memories that you need to remember will come back as needed.
The rest of the thoughts were not necessary.

You may be dealing with heavy emotions from the news, political views, movie star drama, or someone who you feel did something awful. When you get caught up in your brain loops of paranoia, delusion, and being angry at someone before you even talk with them, you can simply repeat the Hawaiian Prayer below.

This is a way to reset the focus back onto you and releasing YOUR old patterns instead of blaming or judging others for your problems and emotional state. This is not a tool to fix other people.

Repeat the Hawaiian prayer either out loud or in your mind and notice how the negative thinking releases to allow gratitude to step in. You can also search for it on You Tube so you can listen to it repeat for extended time periods or overnight to help you move forward.

The Hawaiian Ho'oponopono prayer

Say this:
I Love You
I'm Sorry
Please Forgive Me
Thank you

I Love You
(refers to the memory or data stored in your mind)

I Am Sorry
(for it being in your experience)

Please Forgive Me
(asking for forgiveness as it is a problem)

Thank You
(giving thanks for its release)

The goal is not to delete your whole hard drive all at once. You can become more aware after each repetition and acknowledge what you feel about the subtle change. After playing this prayer over and over in your mind, you won't have to think as hard about it. After a while, this will be your automatic response to any chaotic or irrational thinking and judgment of others. Your thinking will become rational rather than one random impulsive thought following another.

Overthinking can slow down your healing process after loss. It clouds your judgment and creates confusion and chaos and may lead to blame, guilt and damaged relationships. Ultimately you will have more energy to get through every day if you regularly clear out the excessive thoughts. Thinking takes a lot of energy. Allowing, trusting and acceptance uses very little of your energy reserves. Save your energy for spending time with your loved ones, doing something special for yourself, and only allowing thoughts that are in your highest good.

Rest Stop

My favorite essential oils for anxiety and overthinking:
- Lavender
- Geranium
- Bergamot
- Lemon
- German Chamomile

Simply smelling the oils will curb anxiety and overthinking in your brain and improve your mood. You can add oils to a diffuser as well.

You can buy essential oils in your local health food store or online. My favorite online websites are www.rockymountainoils.com and www.mountainroseherbs.com. Or, find your local essential oil representatives from Young Living or DoTerra to assist you with how to use them.

I choose to stay on the road that leads to my joy. Whatever is in my highest good is my priority. I know that will give me strength and courage to deal with people around me more kindly and compassionately.

Chapter 4
Test Drive New Words

"Give sorrow words.
The grief that does not speak knits up the
over wrought heart and bids it break."
~ William Shakespeare, *Macbeth*

When I was a dementia unit manager, one of the residents named Joe was yelling at someone and threw his walker across the room. Hearing the pandemonium, I ran out of my office to see him yelling accusations and punching at the air. He was obviously having a hallucination or memory lapse. I took a breath and mindfully listened to his erratic verbalizations. I heard the word "bully" somewhere in the gibberish, so I played along. I went up to Joe, outstretched my arm and told him to step back. "I got this, Joe. You don't have to worry about this bully anymore." I created a show of beautifully improvised "punching like a girl" and yelling at these fiends to leave Joe alone! I imagined them running madly away from my wrath. Right after I told Joe they were gone, he sighed, sat down and was his old peaceful self.

The act of yelling at Joe's bullies demonstrate how our words matter and make an impact, good or bad. I could have easily told the nurse to get a psychotropic drug to calm him down and tell him that he was having a hallucination. But instead, I yelled emphatically to the bullies that were not there. Those words, albeit said to no one, made a difference.

The frequency of words also matter. Dr. Masaru Emoto, author of the book *Hidden Messages of Water*, is a Japanese scientist who studies our connection with water. He started studying snowflakes to determine why each and every one is completely unique. In doing so, he discovered that water responds to good and bad energy through vibration. It also shows how words have an impact on our reality.

When he first exposed water to happy words, prayers, music and photographs, he froze a small amount of that water. When he looked at it under his microscope, he noticed beautiful, shining, snowflake crystals forming. Each crystal was unique because the water had an energetic vibration.

Conversely, when he exposed the water to sad words, music, and photographs, the water vibrated differently. It didn't form into crystals at all.

To see the crystals for yourself, go to: www.masaru-emoto.net/english/water-crystal.html.

Humans are made of 70% water. It's no wonder we feel heavy and discombobulated when we are around negative people or situations. However, when we are around positive people and situations, we feel light because our bodies are resonating with the States of Being (e.g. Love, compassion, forgiveness) through crystallization. This is similar to the water being exposed to positive words.

I have to assume that something similar happens to the cells in our bodies with positive or negative vibrations. So, going back The States of Being Chart in Chapter One, the heavy emotions such as blame, guilt and fear lead to organs, glands and muscles working less efficiently. This could result in pain, stiffness, digestive issues, and other physical ailments.

On the flip side, when we feel happy, even if we have pain, it feels less intense and the world around us doesn't seem so burdensome.

If you are grieving right now, you may feel stuck in the illusion of what life could have been, or what it will be now after your loss. But that's okay. When you feel this way, embracing the illusion is simply acknowledging that you are considering that healing is possible.

The words you say, illusion or not, are extremely impactful. If you use stronger positive words related to the States of Being instead of the lower states of emotions, whether you believe them or not, they create momentum, which automatically triggers emotional healing. The best part is that it shifts your thinking your emotional state within seconds or minutes.

But, how can your words help your grief or stress? It's a concept I call:

DO, BE, KNOW versus try, should, think

You don't have to believe it to say it.	
Committed High Vibration Truth	Non-Committed Low Vibration Excuses
DO	Try
BE	Should
KNOW	Think
I do one thing to feel better every day.	I'm trying to feel better
I am sad today.	I should feel better by now.
I know I will heal eventually.	I think that I can heal someday.
Peace. Love, Joy "I AM READY TO..."	**Hope "I CAN'T....."**

To always be intending to make a new and better life,
but never to find time to set about it, is as to put off
eating, drinking and sleeping from one day to the next
until you're dead.
~ Og Mandino

Speak the words in the chart. The point of test driving new words is that you can get a sense of which words are in your highest good and which ones halt your progress. Let's talk about the right side of the table above. These words are non-committal because you could say them all day long, but they don't do anything to help you move forward. In fact, if you say them out loud, your voice takes on a more whining tone. This is because these phrases don't align with your highest good, which is your truth. This type of thinking and speaking is a kind of denial about your true emotional state. In saying these words, you *feel* like you are doing something to heal, but you are not doing anything really but procrastinating on taking action. To change the course of your healing process, tell the truth. The left column contains the strong words Do, Be, and Know that bring your true feelings forth. See the examples below:

Instead of:
    I'm trying to feel better.
    I should feel better.
    I think I can heal someday.

Be honest and say:
    I know that I'm not healed yet.
    I do not know how I feel.
    I am still feeling sad.

With strong words, you're laying your cards on the table for all to see. You're just showing people your hand. That's all. There's no judgment in saying what's really happening. Also, you're committing to create a habit in your brain to tell the truth, instead of allowing delusional thinking to take over and pull you back down into sadness or despair.

Instead of:
    I need to feel better.
    I want to heal someday.

Set an intention for healing by saying:
    I am ready to feel better.
    I am ready to heal.
    I am ready to feel happy.

When you say you *need* to feel better, this indicates that you feel bad or perhaps ashamed if you're not better. This is a low vibration state of emotion. Saying that you *want* to heal is a passive statement until you take action steps to heal your emotional state. Wanting to heal is just a thought of doing something but there is no plan for how. However, at least to *want* to do something implies that you're building up the courage think about change.

"I am ready" is so much more powerful! Just like troops that stand ready to go into battle, you stand ready to move ahead one step at a time. It means you're committed to the cause of heading forward toward joy instead of swimming in the swamp of guilt.

The flip side of "I am ready" is that you can say it to empower yourself whether you believe you're ready or not because it bypasses the Ego so that the Soul can take over. The Ego is scared when you want to change. It's the one that keeps you in trying and should mode and fogs up the view ahead. The Soul opens up a path so you can see where you're going—to Joy!

Rest Stop

Catch the lies and dramatic exaggerations you tell yourself.
- Do you say, "I'm starving," instead of "I'm hungry?"
- Do you say, "I'm freezing," instead of "I'm cold?"
- Do you say, "I'm burning up," instead of "I'm feeling hot?"
- Do you say, "I'm fine," when you're not?
- Do you say, "This is taking forever," when this is actually just taking longer than expected?

If you were your brain, imagine the stress and panic you would feel if it thinks your body is starving freezing, or burning! Or, that a task will take forever when it knows that's impossible! The brain can't handle physical harm, unknowns and thoughts that have no resolution. As a result, the tidal waves of irrational thoughts rush in to solve the crisis, chaos ensues, and it has to call in the National Guard to calm the riots.

Therefore it's important to **recognize and replace.** When you say something extreme, immediately ask yourself what the real truth is and say that instead. For example, I catch myself saying "This is taking forever," when I get bored with a task. It verges into the realm of complaining, whining, and frustration. All of these are cousins of the low vibration states of emotions.

After months of practice and new habit forming, I catch myself when I think or say this, backpedal, then replace that statement with "This is taking longer than expected." The reason it is getting easier is that when I say what's really happening, my body relaxes, and I feel mentally and physically relieved. This kind of calm is what happens when the body, mind and soul are in alignment.

According to motivational speaker, Tony Robbins, suffering comes from three words: Loss, Less (comparing yourself to others) and Never (doom and gloom of not getting or doing what you want). The extreme words such as never, always, forever, and hopeless, create an unreachable, impossible goal, which through saying them, increases stress and guilt. For example,

- My life will *never* be the same.
- This *always* happens to me.
- This is *hopeless*!

When you say these extreme words, the subconscious brain records this message and will follow suit with thoughts and emotions that mirror your emotional state. This creates a flood of overthinking that washes out your positivity and hope leaving you feeling regret and apathy. That is, until you flip flop the extreme drama with truth.

- My life is different now without my mother.
- This happened. What else is possible? Or, What am I going to do about it?
- This situation is hard to deal with right now.

Once you start telling yourself the truth on a regular basis, incredible words may start cropping up in your vocabulary. At the least, when someone asks you how you are doing, you might say, "I'm actually good today!" Or, at the most, "I am blissfully happy, thank you!" How do you feel when you say words like this? Probably, amazing! And probably a smile shows up without you even knowing it!

My husband and I both work, so when we're at home in the evenings we feel a bit tired. However, we don't want to condition our 8-year-old daughter, Summer, to be negative. Before, we used to say "We're tired, so please get ready for bed." Now we tell her, "We had an awesome day! We want you to have an awesome day too tomorrow. Get ready for bed so you can get a good night's sleep." Naturally there's a lot less resistance.

Exercise 1

Try out new words

- When people ask you how you are doing
    "I am _____."
- Here is a list of words to choose from, or you can find your own:
    Focused, present, certain, loved, capable, grateful, courageous, wonderful, exuberant, peaceful, kind, radiant, beautiful, boundless, confident, unbeatable, awesome, amazing
- What words are you saying to yourself?
- What would it take to try on the above words and see how they fit?
- When you are feeling tired or worn down, use an exuberant word and say:

"I am _____!" into the mirror or your phone.

Use high vibration extraordinary words on texts, emails, and social media posts personally and professionally. Do people respond more positively?

Are you starting to see how easy it is to shift how you feel and how you affect others more positively despite your emotional state? Isn't it amazing that in seconds or minutes you can go from despair to peace without having to put out tiring effort? Who would have guessed that words can impact our reality so much?

Exercise 2

Feeling your Words

- As you go through the day, be aware of how often you say,
  "I'm trying to _____."
  "I should _____."
  "I think_____."
  Gauge how you feel after you say any of these.
- Set an intention to **recognize and replace** the weak words with a DO, BE or KNOW statement immediately afterwards.
- For example, you might be telling yourself, "I'm trying to lose weight." Instead, you could say something like, "I am ready to lose weight." Or, "I know that I'll feel more energetic if I lose weight." This is what the transformation from weak to strong words look like.
- How do the should, try, think words feel different than the Do, Be Know, words?

> - Set an intention that your brain will be triggered to recognize when you say try, should, or think, a space in your mind automatically opens up for you to replace it with a Do, Be, or Know statement.

If vs. When

- There is a huge difference in meaning when you say if versus when.
  - If I ever feel better, then I will travel.
  - When I feel better, I will travel.

It's obvious which sentence will take you on a trip. Even if you decide not to go on that trip, using the word "when" sets an intention of future thinking and possibilities. It also creates a new habit of your power to create your own reality. When you say "when" over and over, you empower your mind to believe that what you said is going to happen.

It's important to pick your words wisely to avoid misunderstandings. When I was a junior in college, I invited my Hungarian friend to my house in Yukon, Oklahoma for Thanksgiving. He was an avid runner, so he asked where to go to get a run in before dinner. My Mom explained to him that there's a four mile square, which should take him about an hour to run it. After awhile, we all noticed it was dark and Attilla wasn't back yet, so my Mom and I got into the car to search for him.

We lived in the country, so after dark there were no street lights, only moon light. Finally, on a dirt road we found Attilla, and he was extremely relieved to see us. Turns out our neighbors saw this sweaty Hungarian at their door and didn't help him. We don't have a lot of eastern Europeans running around the wheat fields. When we told him about the four-miles square, he thought we meant it was four miles on each side, not four miles total, so he was on his way to finishing 2/3 marathon. This emphasizes the importance of clarification and assuming that the other person may not understand what we are saying. Sometimes when you open up and tell people how you feel about your grief, you might be perturbed when their response is not what you expected. Then you might feel angry or misunderstood. But to change your emotional response, it's important to stay away from assuming that they will know what to say or do.

"The experience is presented to experience it fully. While you're feeling it, choose the healthiest part of your personality to respond."
~Gary Zukav, The Seat of the Soul

First, it's important you clarify what your expectations are to that person. For example, "I simply need someone to listen. I don't want advice." Second, you cannot assume that people understand what you are going through. Even though I've worked with hundreds of hospice patients and their families, I still freeze up sometimes when I talk with the family after their loved one dies. In this case, I'm dealing with my own sadness and confusion, so my responses to them is ladled with awkward I'm sorry's, and too many how are you holding ups. Third, you cannot change the perception of the people around you, but you can change the way you react to their responses. One way to neutralize an awkward situation is to imagine what that person's heart is saying instead. Then with compassion you can gently thank them. To do this, create a state of loving kindness by saying, "May I Be" statements in your head. In doing this, you turn off the need to judge and take what they say personally. In asking permission, you turn it back on yourself to shift to a State of Being akin to love, peace, compassion and joy.

Here are some examples:
- May I be forgiving (if the words from her don't meet my expectations)
- May I be compassionate (to my friend who cares about me)
- May I be gracious (because she wants to support me)
- May I receive love from this person without judgment

Then you can say "May you be..." statements in your head to those around you. For example,
- May you be loved

- May you be at peace
- May you feel my gratitude for being my friend/family member
- May you find peace in the midst of my pain

In doing this, you essentially bestow blessings on that person instead of annoyance and disappointment. No matter how well you attempt to hide these types of reactions, the people around us can feel it. The "May I/You Be" statements create where they can feel the shift of peace and love from you to them. The best part is that even if you are in emotional turmoil or dealing with a chaotic situation, this calms the energy around you as well as your own. It's okay to tell the truth to yourself, or when people ask you how you're are doing after a loss. Much of the time we are not "fine," if we're grieving. It's okay to say, "This fucking sucks!" Or, "This is bull shit!" Or, "I hate this!" The important thing is that pretending to be happy or "fine" can make our lives easier on the outside, but on the inside, the rage, guilt, anxiety, and the other heavy emotions compress and compact deeper into your body and soul. If you feel uncomfortable "losing it" with your family or friends, you can say words like this in the comfort of your own home, or in your car when you're alone.

When you express truly how hard it is, be aware of how you feel afterwards. Do you feel relief? Sadness? Do you feel lighter or heavier? Empowered? Energized? Tired? At this point, it would be good to incorporate the positive words from Exercise 2 in this chapter to neutralize your stress and tension.

Here are some affirmations for you to say when you are feeling uncertain or overwhelmed. Pick out one or two that resonate with you the most.

I trust my inner wisdom and intuition.
This situation is working out for my highest good.
I replace my anger with understanding and compassion.
I trust myself to make the best decision for me.
I surround myself with people that treat me well.
I release my mind of thought until morning.
I wake up to joy every moment.

I let go of worries that drain my energy.
I press on because I believe in my path.

Incorporate these strategies every day and before you know it, you'll feel that your life can have ease. You have the power to shift how you deal with it by the words you say and think.

Chaos happens regardless, but you can transcend
it. Before you know it, your everyday life will become
lighter and lighter. But, first, it's important to step back
from your life and restore your soul.

Chapter 4.5
<u>R.E.S.T.</u> Protocol

Congratulations! You've made it to the halfway point! You are now ready for a R.E.S.T. before the rest of the journey!

> *He restores my soul. He leads me in the paths of righteousness for his name's sake.*
> ~David, Psalm 23:3, The Bible

About two weeks after I came up with the RESTORE JOY acronym for this book, it dawned on me that the first four letters in restore are REST. In the previous four chapters, there was a focus on unconventional ways to shift your thoughts, attention, actions, and words as well how you perceive and interact with others and the world around you. Implementing these strategies brings forth a significant paradigm shift from your previous life.

Even though this is an integral part of your path to healing and joy, changing the way you think, and feel can be exhausting. It's important to let all of those concepts sink in as you begin to let go of your previous patterns and start looking to what is ahead. You are now closer to peace, love, and joy than before, and the journey ahead will start getting easier. But for now, the *need for rest*.

Rest allows you to step away from real life for a while to get some understanding of what life is all about. At this point in your journey, what and who with whom you surround yourself or what you see in the media or on the internet won't be as important anymore. It's the world inside of you, your North Star, your soul, which lays out your upcoming journey despite what happened in the past.

Here is the R.E.S.T. Protocol to incorporate in when you feel overwhelmed, emotional, or depleted.

The R.E.S.T. protocol

R – Remember to Breathe

Chest Squeeze
Place the knuckles from one had on the palm under the fingers on the other hand. Hold gently for 10 seconds to 1 minute, then switch. Be aware of your chest muscles releasing tension or easier breathing.

Prayer Hold
Put your hands in a light prayer hold in front of your heart or in your lap. Hold it for 10 seconds to 1 minute. Be aware of how you feel emotionally when you are done.

E – Ease into Center

Hand Hug
Lightly place your fingers into the palm of your hand and hold for 10 seconds to 3 minutes to nurture yourself or sleep better.

S - Sit in Peace
Be an observer instead of a judger. This allows you to see other people with curiosity and acceptance instead of someone with a problem that must be solved.

T – Time Out
Create a space or nook of peace wherever you are.

When David writes about God restoring his soul in Psalms 23, he is referring to how shepherds bring back sheep who have wandered away and keep them from wandering aimlessly. Your mind may seem to wander constantly leading to distraction and procrastination from the important stuff. Rest is one antidote for a straying mind. It's about sitting still enough so you don't get caught up in worries and micromanaging everyday life.

I'm the Queen of Straying and an expert escape artist. In my 20's and early 30's I would literally move to different parts of the U.S. to avoid dealing with people or situations that were hurtful or embarrassing. I was like Julia Roberts in the *Runaway Bride* where life was good until any kind of commitment or confrontation was required.

I was happy with life overall until a harsh reality hit me like an egg in my face. The problem was that I only trusted my Ego more than I trusted God. As a result, I found myself making impulsive decisions that were not in my highest good and ultimately led to suffering and emotional turmoil after heart breaks and hurt feelings. I was not on the right path for my highest good.

When David refers to "leading me in the path of righteousness," there is no danger of getting hurt, feeling weary, or wandering away because this path is safe. Of course, David was referring to his walk with God, but in the same way, you are on the path following your own soul to get to the true essence of peace, joy, and love.

When I allowed myself to trust the guidance of the shepherd (God and my soul), I could be still for awhile, rooted and settled, no matter what life threw my way. I finally felt safe and taken care of. I finally realized I didn't have to rebuild the parts of the life that kept falling down. My path was to find a life structure that is solid.

Creating Ceremony: Taking time to honor your loss and the journey ahead.

When I lived in Thailand, I was excited to go my first Buddhist Ceremony. My Thai little sisters and I walked into a large open area with a small temple in the middle and sat down in the grass. There were jungle sounds in the background, a warm breeze and a clear starry night sky. I was exhilarated by the sum of all this wonderfulness. Then it started.

My friends told me to kneel and put my hands in a prayer hold next to my heart. The ceremony started. It was all spoken in Thai, in which I was nowhere near to fluent. But I watched and smiled at the whole scene. It was otherworldly and there was a collective peace. But then 15 minutes went by, 30 minutes, 45 minutes. My knees were crying out in ultimate stiffness and discomfort. Americans are not conditioned to kneel for long periods of time. I was getting antsy. I couldn't understand the words so I was unsure of what they were teaching us. I was getting hungry. I didn't know how long these ceremonies lasted so I was totally unsure of what was next.

Anxiety started creeping from my head into my body. I was restless and nervous while my friends were totally engaged. Finally, after three days, well, actually 15 more minutes, the ceremony ended, my friends handed me a lotus flower and a candle and they said, "Joy, we will light your candle then you just walk around the temple three times."

My anxiety turned to utter joy! This was going to be so easy and fast, then we can go eat! So, I walked around the temple as fast as possible. I was going to win this race. I just knew it. But my candle went out. So, I walked quickly back to my friends, relit my candle, then strived for the finish line with two more laps to go. My candle went out two more times, but my friends relit it anyway.

Once I sped around for the third round, my dear sweet little Thai sisters, Maew and Sine, smiled and walked slowly up to me. Quietly they said "Joy, the reason for this ceremony was to keep light on in your heart, and yours kept going out." Boy, did I feel like a cad."

Almost two decades later, I still hold onto the lesson of slowing down, being in the moment, and realizing that ceremony holds beauty and meaning for how to move forward gracefully and gratefully.

Therefore, honoring yourself through ceremony can give you insights that are different from reading information about healing or thinking out solutions on your own. It's active, not passive. Also, ceremony sets an intention that you are ready to embrace what it would take to free yourself of heaviness and emotional pain.

By creating your own ceremony, you will find the way to stock your shelves with cans and jars of love, peace, joy, forgiveness, awareness, and other States of Being. Then, when you are struggling, you can go to the shelves and grab what you need or what you want to give to others. It goes back to the awareness that you don't have to create the States of Being for you to experience them. They are simply there waiting to be used and expressed.

Ceremony is an ideal time to find a refuge or safe haven where you can retreat. It can be in your home or yard, or you can travel somewhere that offers your peace and solace. It's important, especially after a major life event such as losing a loved one or any other major loss, that you treat yourself to being in solitude, and then "re-treat" on a regular basis by yourself or with others. If you allow yourself to retreat away from everyday life, the clouds around you will clear so you can truly see the beauty of your soul and your purpose despite what's happened to you.

Being alone can be scary at first if you spend a lot of time helping others before yourself. Therefore, it's important to treat yourself gently and kindly. You do deserve to get to know yourself. In the end, others will be blessed by your gifts as they rise up to the surface.

The key is to wrap the treating yourself experience around anything that makes your heart sing and gives you a glimpse of happiness and peace. If solitude and withdrawing does not resonate with you, then you may be more content instead being with others who are also experiencing a similar loss to yours. For some, being around people who are not going through your experience may be more healing.

Rest Stop

Here are some suggestions for treating yourself:

- Go out for a latte or some ice cream for an hour
- Visit your favorite café, book shop, or store
- Do some gardening
- Buy new kitchen gadget or art supply you've been wanting
- Write a wish list of things or experiences that only you

would use or do. Look at it daily and imagine what life would look like if you did one of them.

- Set up a sacred corner or room in your house where you feel peaceful and safe
- Go to a movie alone

Walking in the lotus: A ceremony for slowing down

In 2002, my friend Julie and I went to the Getty Museum in Los Angeles. Amidst all of the thousand-year-old relics and classic art, there is a walking trail in the middle. There was so much to see in our short time there, I was frantically and impatiently walking around older and younger people alike to experience the trail before heading to the next section. Julie, a social worker, pulled me aside and told me how crazy I looked rushing through an area that was supposed to be calming. So, she gave me an exercise to slow down.

With each step, I was to imagine stepping into a lotus flower. During the first step while I was rolling my eyes, I slowly stepped in. Then after the second step, my eyes lifted up to the beautiful architecture of the museum and the clear blue sky. As I continued, I noticed my breathing grew from the first releasing sigh to an even rhythm.

Before walking mindfully, I hadn't even noticed the beauty of my surroundings or how the other visitors were taking in this awesome experience. From that point on, I took my time and not only observed the beauty, but felt it down to my soul.

Exercise 1

Mindful Walking

Anytime you walk at home or at work, practice mindful walking to slow down overthinking and rest into the peace of the moment. With each step, be aware of planting your foot before you take a step with the next one. Use this mantra to help.

First comes the little toe.
Then comes the big toe.
Then comes the heel.
And then take a step.

As you mindfully walk, look up and around. Is there someone or something you didn't notice before slowing down?

Mindful Tasking

Instead of thinking of all of the tasks you have on your to do list, just do one at a time.
- Count down from 10 to 1.
- Take a breath.
- Take off your worry backpack that contains all your tasks.
- Leave it at the door.
- Take mindful steps toward your task or errand.
- Simply do the task because it is the only one on your list right now.

From here on out, after "R.E.S.T.-ing", the focus will be on restoring your soul, particularly listening to it instead of your head. Doing this ultimately gets you closer to your ultimate goal: joy.

Rest is the body's way of stepping back from
chaos and stress to recharge. Then you will
have the power and momentum to get through
the rest of your day, week, year, or life.

Chapter 5:
Overcome Negativity

"How did you fall in, Eeyore?" asked Rabbit, as he dried
  him with Piglet's handkerchief.
"I didn't," said Eeyore.
"But how–"
"I was BOUNCED," said Eeyore.
"Oo," said Roo excitedly, "Did somebody push you?"
"Somebody BOUNCED me. I was just thinking by the
  side of the river–thinking, if any of you know what that
  means–when I received a loud BOUNCE."
"Oh, Eeyore!" said everybody.
"Are you sure you didn't slip?" asked Rabbit wisely.
"Of course I slipped. If you're standing on the slippery
  bank of a river, and somebody BOUNCES you loudly
  from behind, you slip. What did you think I did?"
  ~ (Eeyore), A.A. Milne, The House at Pooh Corner

Poor, Eeyore, the good-hearted, glum blue donkey from the Winnie
the Pooh book series. He gets rained on. He gets "bounced" into
a river by Tigger, who is the epitome of optimism as well as spon-
taneous, and occasionally reckless, fun. It seems Eeyore just can't
catch a break.

However, his lot in life is self-inflicted. He has been down in the
dumps mentally for so long, his depressed personality is a constant
in Pooh Corner.

People who are in the midst of grief or a major life change may
feel like Eeyore slipping into a river. He's defensive and corrects his

friends who are trying to help him. His words display the infamous wanting to be told that he's right and the other person is wrong to feel worthy or validated.

He's also intent on justifying that he was bounced and that it wasn't his fault that he slipped in. Eeyore kept saying how he was bounced by Tigger and thereby placing blame on Tigger for his emotional state. This is the epitome of blame, unworthiness, powerlessness and the expectation that negativity will just keep happening.

The Toll Negativity Takes

After grief or any kind of major life change, like Eeyore, it's easy to fall into negativity and defensiveness. The emotional world of dark clouds is similar to having S.A.D., Seasonal Affective Disorder. Without light, or lightness, the storm seems to have no end. You might feel tired, listless, or unmotivated which fuels further negativity.

> *"Leading behavioral researchers have told us that as much as seventy-seven percent of everything we think is negative, counterproductive, and works against us. At the same time, medical researchers have said that as much as seventy-five percent of all illnesses are self-induced."*
> ~ Shad Helmstetter, *What to Say When you Talk To Yourself*

When positive, optimistic people come around, it's natural to be a bit envious that they're happy and you're not, even if they're friends or family coming to help. Or, you might feel over-stimulated or overwhelmed when they tell you that it's time to start being happy again when you're not ready.

Then, there are days when you may feel you just can't get out of your emotional pain or grief. Last Thanksgiving, one of my family members had a coffee cup that said, "I can't even" on it. This phrase is almost a laughable joke about how if we're going through stress, we put our fists in the air and say, "I can't even!!" as a way to cope.

But, I saw it in a different light during Thanksgiving dinner. My

Mom was drinking coffee out of that cup, and as "I can't even" went up to her mouth, I saw the unrelenting stress and grief in her eyes as a result of the major losses she experienced the prior 18 months. She experienced a major medical event where she could have died, and she and my Dad had to sell their dream house in the country to move to a senior living community. My Mom sadly watched some of her belongings in her house being shuffled out to a dumpster because she couldn't fit 3000 square feet of things into a 1000 square foot cottage.

So, now, when I see anything saying, "I can't even," I feel sad. And my own grief of her pain resurfaces. Then I get grouchy, negative, and pissed off at the world. You may also have similar triggers that lead you to a path of negativity and complaining as a coping mechanism.

My Mom has so many reasons to complain about her new life, but she's found peace with it because she finally came to the point of acceptance of her situation. Complaining takes you nowhere but to negativity.

> "To complain is always non-acceptance of what I…. When you complain, you make yourself into a victim. When you speak out, you are in your power. So, change the situation by taking action, or by speaking out if necessary or possible; leave the situation or accept it. All else is madness."
> ~Eckhart Tolle, *The Power of Now: A Guide to Spiritual Enlightenment*

Even if you've had some hard times in your life recently or in the past, is it worth it to complain about how bad your life is? It may spread bad energy, keep you stuck, and leave you powerless to change.

Overcoming this type of negative thinking is a step toward changing your thoughts, mindset, and heart set. Acceptance of all that has happened to you takes you to the State of Being having to do with harmony, forgiveness, and transcending your negative emotions.

It's hard for Negativity to exist where forgiveness lives.

Feeling negative or hopeless not only affects your health and emotional state, but also affects everyone around you, including animals and plants. According a study from the book, *The Power of Prayer on Plants*, by Franklin Loehr, one set of seeds received positive prayer, while the other set of seeds received negative prayer. Here are the results:

- Positive prayer helped speed the growth and germination of the seeds
- The seeds which received positive prayer produced more vigorous plants
- Negative prayers halted the growth of the plants

Similarly, in *Healing Oils, Healing Hands*, Linda Smith explains how negative thoughts or people lower the frequency of our energy field by 12 MHz (megahertz). This is when your energy level may feel low, tired, or unmotivated. This explains why we feel heavy or depressed after a bout with negativity.

To put this in perspective, the normal range of a healthy body is 62-68 MHz. If you allow negative thoughts or people to come near you, your frequency lowers below 62 MHz, which increases your susceptibility to things like colds and flu. Over time, negativity will continue to decrease your energy level, which potentially could lead to serious illness.

Rest Stop

How to protect yourself from emotional vampires— people who suck out your positive energy, according to the book *Positive Energy* by Judith Orloff.
- Break eye contact to stop transfer of negative energy
- Vacuum Breathing

- Take a deep breath and take back every drop of positive energy you lost
- Exhale negative vibes out of the lower spine
- Envision black gunk leaving your body
- Breathe in fresh air

If you're around a lot of emotional vampires at once:
- Find a quiet area, take a deep breath, and close your eyes
- Visualize tranquil setting like a meadow or ocean then participate with all five senses
- Stay there until you feel centered
- Go back into the real world

Take special care of yourself around people in need:
- Compassion without too much empathy
- Be well fed & rested when you're in the presence of needy or sick people
- Hug, but don't hang on
- Walk around the room to de-intensify contact
- When you leave, recharge yourself
- Shake your hands to release any negativity you received from that person

Footnote: People who are ill have a lower body frequency than people who are healthy. As a result, they inadvertently attract other people's positive energy. If you work around sick people, or take care of someone who is sick, be sure and use some of the strategies above, or ask Archangel Michael to protect you from negative energy before you're in their presence.

Linda Smith also points out there are ways to increase your energy level to improve your health and your emotional state.

Change Your Energy Field and Restore Balance

Prayer
1.Prayers and meditation raised frequency by 15 MHz

Energy Healing
2. Positive thoughts raised frequency by 10 MHz

Essential Oils
3. Smelling essential oils raises your body frequency immediately

Essential oil frequencies are coherent with health frequencies in your body unlike synthetic fragrances and pharmaceuticals
A negative self-image can lead to anxiety, depression, and other low frequency emotions.
Consider eating and drinking higher frequency foods and beverages to raise your body frequency to a healthier level. This includes organic foods, fruits, vegetables, herbs, humanely raised meats, superfoods, and spices such as cloves, ginger, basil, and thyme

Rest Stop

Using Solfeggio Frequencies for Healing

On YouTube, iTunes, and Amazon music, there are many videos and sound recordings with different Solfeggio frequencies. Almost every night, I go to sleep to the 528 Hz frequency flowing through my ear buds. I can literally feel my energy unblocking before I fall into a deep sleep. But you can look up which of the frequencies below resonate with what you're going through.

396 Hz - Liberating Guilt and Fear
417 Hz - Undoing Situations and Facilitating Change
528 Hz - Transformation and Miracles (DNA Repair)
639 Hz - Connecting/Relationships
741 Hz - Awakening Intuition
852 Hz - Returning to Spiritual Order

Knowing the frequency ranges reiterates how important it is to reduce negativity, so you can easily rise to forgiveness and other States of Being. When I hold group medium events, I have cardboard bricks representing the Scale of Consciousness. Blame is at the bottom and God is at the top. Every time I remove blame, guilt, and the other levels off the string, a helium balloon goes higher and higher. When I take off the final brick, the balloon floats effortlessly up to the ceiling.

Moreover, once you release your heavy emotions and negativity, you automatically start feeling content and happier with ease. Happiness is not something that has to be forced. It's simply like the sun sitting behind the dark clouds of your negativity.

> *"What we focus on, we empower and enlarge. Good multiplies when focused upon. Negativity multiplies when focused upon. The choice is ours: Which do we want more of?"*
> –Julia Cameron, *Blessings*

There is **HOPE!**
Hold On Pain Ends

I love this acronym! It implies perseverance and faith. There is light at the end of the tunnel, even if you can't see it yet. Fred Luthans and his colleagues compiled a psychological framework that includes hope called Psychological Capital (PsyCap). It's a higher order construct composed of 4 underlying pieces which make you a **HERO**:

Hope (proactively planning goals)
Self-Efficacy (confidence)
Resilience (successfully coping with adversity or stress)
Optimism (being positive about succeeding now and in the future)

The following outcomes are based on 51 empirical investigations when workers in organizations displayed positive PsyCap qualities

include:
- Job satisfaction
- Commitment to the organization
- Psychological well-being
- Citizenship

When employees displayed undesirable behaviors, this led to the follow negative outcomes:
- Cynicism
- Turnover
- Job stress
- Anxiety

The workers who were positive and optimistic were invested in doing their job well. They made a choice to enjoy work.

Are you ready to be invested in your happiness, instead of negativity and drama? What would it take to enjoy life, even while you grieve, or while life creates stress around you?

One way to achieve this is through the Loving Kindness Meditation below. Although, many Buddhists have a formal meditation practice with this concept, these strategies can easily be applied to bring forth compassion toward yourself, others, and everyone in the world. Be aware of your emotions and any tension in your body. Then say or think the following:

Loving Kindness Meditation
May I be filled with lovingkindness.
May I be safe from inner and outer dangers.
May I be well in body and mind.
May I be at ease and happy.

How do your mind, emotions and body feel after saying it? Next say the same meditation to others.

"May you be...."

Lastly, say it to everyone in the world.

"May everyone be...."

Some benefits of this practice include:
- Increased positive emotions
- Decreased migraines and chronic pain
- More empathy
- Relaxation
- Increased compassion and empathy
- Less self-criticism
- Decreased anger

This can also be adapted to any negative situation or person in your life. For example, it might be easy to say, "May you be filled with loving kindness" to someone you're thankful for, or who has helped you.

However, would it be challenging for you to say it someone you don't like or who you're having a hard time with?

Whether it is or not, you can feel empowered sending love to people who make you miserable. In doing this, you no longer are in a state of judgment of what that person should or shouldn't do. Instead, you're choosing to say high vibration words that break the barrier of scorn.

Just by saying these words, you create a peacefulness around yourself in which you can see others, yourself, and your grief in the light of love and compassion. There's no emotional baggage in Loving Kindness. Then you can be in a peaceful space to look at your past with curiosity instead of judgment.

Always remember, you deserve positive people and expe-riences in your life. Keep yourself healthy physically and emotionally to attract positivity wherever you are.

Chapter 6
<u>R</u>emember then Look Ahead

"Sometimes memories sneak out of my eyes
and roll down my cheeks."
~ Unknown

There's a famous movie from 1957 called The Bridge over the River Kwai. I've never seen the movie, but I've rafted down the notorious river. Quite honestly, as I was standing on a bamboo raft with a long bamboo pole in hand to row, I was pondering and visualizing the mournful 1927 Mississippi River African American ballad "Ole Man River" from the musical Showboat. Or, how the elegant gondoliers must feel floating through the canals of Venice. But I was snapped back to reality when I was splashed by my Thai high school sophomores that were swimming along on either side as I kept the raft going straight instead of off to dream land. Nevertheless, I was very excited to be on the same river that the Japanese wanted the British POW's to build a bridge over so they could continue their Indochina domination. It's historical, you know.

It's a good thing to remember and cherish our memories. They shape us. They make us smile or cry. And they chronicle our lives, history, loved ones, and people met along the way.

However, the reality in front of us still exists and has to be dealt with. Memories are good in a time of rest, but in a time of action can take us off course. The present moment beckons something from us and now we must look at what lies ahead and further upstream to determine what else is possible.

Have you noticed the far off look people who are reminiscing have? Having worked with persons with dementia for over 20 years, I've seen that gaze in almost everyone with mid to late stage Alzheimer's disease. The long-term memories are intact, but the short-term memories are elusive or gone. They gaze out at the recent and far past memories, which gets farther and farther away each day. But that's all they have.

You, on the other hand, have the capability to set a course ahead based on who you are now after loss. As you see glimpses of hopes or dreams between bouts of grief, it's important to store them away to be retrieved as soon as the opportunity arises to navigate and propel yourself to the next step.

"You can't start the next chapter of your life if you keep reading the last one."
~ Unknown

When I lived in Sacramento, I often rode my bike along shore of the Sacramento River. It was asphalt with a yellow line in the middle. Because I rode this trail so much that I was bored, I rode in the middle to see how long I can keep my front wheel on the yellow line. It was harder than I thought.

For my first few tries, the front wheel zigged and zagged on either side of the line as I set my gaze toward the end of the trail. Then when I looked back to see where my back wheel was, my front wheel went completely off course and I had to put a foot down to keep from falling over. Then I finally found the sweet spot. If I simply looked about two feet in front of my wheel, I could stay on the line almost constantly.

When you look too far ahead of where you are, it's shaky at best. Anticipating a better life ahead is hopeful and motivating, but it doesn't address where you are now in your grief process.

When you look at the past, while simultaneously moving ahead into obligations of everyday life, you have meltdowns, anxiety, periods of being noncommittal and unsure due to unresolved issues.

If you need to deal with raw emotions, regrets, and find ways to forgive what happened, put the brakes on and look back. Once you see what's there and acknowledge that the emotional pain eventually will be released, get back up and ride ahead a bit and see what happens as you keep pedaling.

When you see an hour or a day ahead, life is doable. Expectations become realistic. It's okay if you may not be totally healed by then. But at least you can see the small steps leading to each day getting a little bit easier and better. It feels good to feel steady, even though it's a precarious and often a hard journey. Riding on this road to your joy is the reason to get up every morning. Joy is at the end, and is the perfect soul mate to your sorrow.

So, how do you find balance with remembering the people, job, or lifestyle from the past, with present and future obligations, along with changes? First, it's important to be open to your heart's messages about focusing on the past. When it's time to look at the future, your heart will tell you.

Here's a personal example. One day I was just driving along minding my own business when my rear-view mirror unattached and flew into my lap. My first thought was, how can I drive without a rear view mirror?

My second thought was to thank the powers that be (most likely angels) who probably orchestrated this to demonstrate that I need to focus on moving forward, not backwards into the past. I attempted to reattach the mirror several times to no avail. The benefit of having no rear-view mirror is that you can see a panorama of what's ahead always. I'm not tempted to look behind me, or fix my make-up and hair at stop lights. Instead, now I see sunsets and cloud formations, also known as hope and possibility, in full IMAX view.

Fast forward to April 2017. I was spiraling my rental car around drop off curves, as I drove in circles around the mountain down historic Highway 89 in Northern Arizona. To my disappointment, the rear view mirror blocked my view of the peaks, ridges and trees that I longed to see because of my many trips that way 11 years before. All I could see was the road behind me as I unsafely ducked my head to see the view. That darn mirror! If I look behind, I'll plunge to my death!

My panorama was gone, blemished by a view of my unkempt

hair and half ass make-up job. And so I looked ahead, which was beautiful, but I didn't see the big picture. Only the left and right, not the middle.

Sometimes being stuck in the past and remembrance can lead to missing out the beauty of what's going on right now, or missing important events with family or friends. Looking back may also lead to resentment of things unresolved. This is akin to my car racing down the mountain. I had to be completely focused on what was ahead, or I would crash.

Maybe you have already crashed you were looking behind instead of ahead. Or, perhaps you aren't ready to think about what it would be like to move ahead without a certain person, job, or experience in your life.

Exercise 1

Getting Clarity about Your Future Exercise

Either write or think about the following questions:
- What does my life look like now without that person, job, or experience in my life?
- What else is possible?
- Who am I becoming?
- Are the people with whom I surround myself in my highest good?

In 2001, I had gained about 40 pounds and felt bad about the way I looked. So, as most of us do, or intend to do, I joined a gym. Step aerobics was my go to exercise program. I stood in the front, but I did everything I could to avoid looking at the overweight woman in the mirror. The teacher was great, and the routine was fun, until my last class. There was a sub for some reason.

About 15 minutes into the class, she said to put away the steps. (Uh, this is step aerobics! Hello!) She said she was a jazzercise teacher, so we would do some dance moves to change it up. Then I see the woman do a salsa type move and on the 3 count she slapped her own butt. Seriously, she did. Then, I was appalled when the rest of the class was doing the same. I glared at my "What the hell!" expression in the mirror as the teacher then excitedly told us to get a mat and stand on our heads. With full resolve that this was not in my highest good, I shrugged and walked out of the door to change my reality.

Your life is not the past, even if you fathom that it is. You don't have to deal with other people's crap anymore. You can choose who is in your inner circle now based on who you are now. You don't have to rehash your regrets anymore. Right now, those regrets don't exist.

However, it's important to acknowledge and make peace with the past before you move ahead. Here are some suggestions:

Ways to Remember so You Can Look Ahead
- Honor your loss by creating a bag, shrine, room nook, scrapbook or vision board. Include items that relate to cherished memories such as rocks, photos, trinkets, written words, inspirational quotes or poems.
- Create a daily ceremony, or use some of the suggestions above to honor and envision your new path of who you are now after loss.
- Get an essential oil that reminds you of memories of the person has passed, the good things about any other loss, or that makes you feel peaceful about your upcoming journey.
- Plant something that represents good memories or inspiration for your own growth.

When you stand at the edge of a cliff and look out, you can see for hundreds of miles. Be in tune with how awesome your possibilities look. The past seems small when you see what's ahead.

Chapter 7
Embrace Change

"Everything you've ever wanted is
on the other side of fear."
~ Unknown

"How do geese know when to fly to the sun?
Who tells them the seasons?
How do we, humans know when it is time to move on?
As with the migrant birds, so surely with us, there is a
voice within if only we would listen to it, that tells us
certainly when to go forth into the unknown."
~ Elisabeth Kubler-Rosss

In his book *Waking Up,* Sam Harris addresses how you see change. He writes that when you look at a window, do you see your reflection, or do you see what's outside in the world? Is your focus on your emotional pain from the past or the road ahead to joy?

At this phase of readying yourself for change and to evolve, you may feel vacillation and trepidation of which direction to go emotionally and literally. This is normal. There's a teeter totter of fear and excitement, up and down over and over, until you fully accept that change is inevitable. After all, acceptance leads to lasting change.

Dealing with Loss
This is a personal example of reluctantly letting go. I remember the night clearly. It was around 9pm in late September after my daughter Summer's chaotic third birthday party. I, standing alone in my

driveway, under our 25-foot-high buckeye tree on an unusually clear starry night was homed in on the round red tail lights that minutes before were MY round red tail lights.

My niece and her husband were leaving, driving down Sunset Drive in my white 2000 Volkswagen Peace Beetle I gave to them. How apropos because, after all, this was a sunset moment in my life. A pivotal transition and lesson in un-grasping.

So, I just stood rooted in shock with stinging tears welling up, and a house full of guests laughing and meandering through brightly lit windows, that I had no desire to join them.

As the tears welled up, I reflected how my Beetle was my "coming out" party in 2002. It was me finally acknowledging my "hippie"-ness, poetic and adventurous nature, which ultimately cemented that the spark in me that ignited an inward and outward journey of vagabonding. It also defined my desire to identify the missing "peace" in me, others, and the world.

In 2009, my Peace Beetle, with its wounds and cracks literally Tyvek taped together from years of adventures, nestled my little newborn baby Summer in the back seat safe and sound. And then, my daughter outgrows the back seat. I feel a twinge of the breadth of commitment to my daughter, over my white arched companion that had loyally been there for me through the years!

The loss creeps up from the middle of my chest like a parasite, poking a hole through my sternum causing me to swallow hard and gasp for breath. It was the day of reckoning when I saw her round red lights one final time.

Watching my Beetle drive away was like the feeling after a sunset — the point where the afterglow fades into dark blues and dark grays. The moment when the quiet of night settles in and says to wind down, slow down, settle into the womb, and be reborn when the new day comes. So I did, reluctantly, but I did.

The next morning, I rebelliously dug my heels in as I walked up to the Honda CR-V. I opened the door. I sat behind the wheel with gritted teeth, turned it on, and it drove me forward to that inward place of surrender. I was free.

Change is hard at first, messy in the
middle, and gorgeous at the end.
~ Robin Sharma

It's hard enough to change even if you want to. But, the thought of being forced to change, especially after grief and loss, is daunting and sometimes oppressive.

Heather's experience below is a great example of what to do when change hits you in the face. Heather's husband, Brian, died at the age of 43 from metastatic cancer, leaving behind his wife Heather and their young daughters. Heather and the girls had a painstakingly difficult time through the grief process. After Brian died, she used to come to my office for intuitive medium and healing sessions.

In my sessions, I see and intuit pictures that represent the client's life. During Heather's first appointment, I told her I saw a shack over her right shoulder with no nails that kept falling down into a disheveled pile. After she set the pieces back together, other pieces would fall. Then after several attempts, I saw Heather and her girls leave the broken pieces that hurt so much behind.

Three years after Brian died, Heather sent me this note about her healing journey:

> *"I think of that story often these days because you told me to let them go, and how you saw me walk away with just my kids. That's exactly how it went down. I left all the broken pieces that hurt so much behind, and only took my kids.*
>
> *All those broken pieces that I kept trying so hard to hold weren't mine anymore. Letting go became the only option to move forward."*

The realization that putting the old pieces of her life together was futile, finally fueled Heather to choose a new road for her and her daughters. They're now living happily in Kentucky, in their own home, and she has a successful massage business.

Often, it's hard to find someone else who understands what you're going through, especially when it comes to moving forward after loss. Ultimately, who knows you better than yourself.

In 2007, I was struggling with the grief of moving to Illinois the year before, and dealing with a job that I wasn't happy with. The relationship between my live in boyfriend and I was challenged because my grief and anxiety were so heavy. But Ellen Lerner, my life coach, gave me a wonderful tool to get some answers.

She said to imagine myself 20 years from now and ask future Joy how to solve these issues. So, in the middle of Starbucks, I closed my eyes as she led a guided meditation and I met peaceful, happy, content 54 year old Joy. She was dressed in comfortable REI clothes, living in a cabin in an aspen forest with three floor to ceiling windows that have full bookshelves in between each one.

The 34-year-old me sat down on her couch and listened as she shared her State of Being. We had a lovely conversation. I don't remember what she said, but I could feel the contentment, peace and ease she lived. Most importantly, she was happy and was not anywhere near the despair I felt. As a result, I could then embrace what was possible for my journey. After all these years, the image of her gives me hope.

The interesting part of this that I didn't realize at the time was that my daughter who was born two years later will graduate from high school when I'm 54.

Rest Stop

Your Future Self

Talk with your future self-one year, five years or ten years from now.
Or, choose your own time frame.

- Sit in a quiet place
- You can just do a meditation where you envision your future self
- Or, you can write in a journal

Imagine with all your senses and see all the vivid details:
- Where does your future self live?
- What does your future self look like?
- How are they doing emotionally?
- What's a typical day and night for your future self?
- Who is with your future self at different times throughout the day?

Have a conversation with your future self.
- Ask questions about how he or she got to this point
- Be aware of how you feel talking with yourself
- Do you feel more confident to embrace change?
- What insights do you receive?

When I see clients in my office, I will often ask that person's Higher Self or Soul Self what's really going on to keep that person from moving forward. Gary Zukav, author of Seat of the Soul, explains how the soul has multisensory perception, which the five senses can't provide. Your brain is the back-seat driver telling the soul where to go, but soul is the driver with an internal GPS that guides the way to your destination: joy.

During appointments with my clients, there are times when it's harder than normal to clear negative energy from the body. So, I ask permission from that person's Soul Self to give me insights on what's really going on beyond what the client told me. In my mind, the Soul Self looks like them, but is often much more relaxed and offers objective viewpoints about what is really causing his or her resistance, stress and anguish versus what my client thinks is going on. It's also like a coach offering specific helpful hints and strategies for letting go of old patterns, releasing emotional pain, and guiding towards positive change.

A huge barrier to change is other people who are stressing us out. Fortunately, you can "talk to" or communicate with their Soul, even if that person is not speaking with you. Whether a person has passed away, or is living, you can have conversations with them without the emotional resistance that might show up when you speak in person.

For example, some of my clients are contemplating divorce because of lack of communication with the spouse. I told them to ask questions or have a conversation with the spouse's higher self, and then patiently be aware of any shifts. Several of them told me that their spouse was more peaceful, calm and open even though they didn't speak with their spouse in person.

Tapping into the Soul Self is just the beginning of finding resolution with the people around us so you can move forward emotionally. Simply tune into that person's higher self and ask them your questions.

The next step is to give up, also known as forgiveness.

Exercise 2

Communicating with Other Higher Self's

Giving Up

- Imagine the worst regrets, worries and fears you have and put them in an imaginary box.
- Visualize the box in your hands.
- Literally lift your hands into the air above your head and give them up to God and the Angels.

Doing this is liberating, dear one. You don't have to carry the burdens anymore.

Likewise, forgiveness does the same. It erases any heavy emotions about the person that you're holding inside of yourself. Then the burdens lift away from you so you can move. These burdens are too heavy for you to carry as you step ahead.

Forgiveness to Restore Your Joy

- In your head or out loud, simply say, "I forgive you" over and over until you feel light.
- It's not necessary to say who or why you are forgiving, or to say it to the person who's done you wrong.
- The simple act of saying "I forgive you" means you're willing to forgive and that you're ready to move forward to a state of love and peace within yourself.
- Saying "I forgive you" means you love yourself enough to let go of hurtful situations and conversations.

Choosing Your Tribe

- Write down what types or the names of people you want around you now, and how they support your road to joy instead of pain.
- Some of the people you have known a long time may not be part of your new tribe. Allow them to fall away on their own. You are a different person now, having forgiven.
- Open yourself up to the possibility of awesome people who will support you now and lift you up.

The Stages of Change

Sometimes you may feel you're ready to change, but don't see any progress. Author Robin Sharma talks about how if you do 1% everyday toward your most important goals, you'll get there in the right time, and with the right wisdom and experience along the way. This takes patience.

My husband, John, is a carpenter and has been renovating our home for 3 years now. When I come home, he explains all of the little things he did to the electrical, walls, floor or lighting to make it look right. Since my attention to detail is very limited, I tell him "That's great, honey." But the truth is I have no clue what he did.

Restoring an old house involves tearing the old stuff out then adding new features while maintaining its original beauty. Similarly, restoring your soul and joy can be a painful and liberating process over time. In the end, there's a peaceful contentment when you look back at what you went through to get to where you are now. Below are some examples of how restoring a grief-ridden heart parallels restoring an old home:

1. Feeling vulnerable and raw
   - The walls were open and ugly with only one inch of plywood to protect us from the cold weather

2. What you want now is different, than what you wanted before your loss.
   - Tearing down walls in basement that made it feel small and closed in
   - Changing the house to what we want, which is different than the needs of the previous owners

3. Finding a new way to function in everyday life now while setting an intention for new "doorways" to present themselves.
   - A piece of plywood was nailed over where the front door should be
   - How do you open a door that's unhinged? Patiently wait for the door to be installed so you can open it easily
   - The only option is to go around to the back to get to the front of the house

4. Peace, love, joy and forgiveness are waiting to be installed once you clear out your old emotional baggage
   - Sinks and desks sit in the basement until the old bathroom and office are torn apart and restored

5. With each step, you can see progress and know it will eventually get done. Give yourself credit for what you've done to move ahead

- Looking at old photos of before the renovations happened to remind yourself that dramatic transformation has already taken place, even though it's not complete

6. Trust your instincts. You know in your heart and gut when a change feels right or wrong

- My husband wants to put dark blue siding on our house. Every time he says that, my stomach seizes up. I know it doesn't resonate. If I don't speak up about this, I'll have to live with that heaviness in my belly every time I look at the house.

Rest Stop

If you were to go skydiving and you jump out of the plane, there's no going back. This exercise allows you to experience what it physically feels like to decide to move forward for good.

Where the nose goes, the body flows

- Stand straight, head forward, with your hands to your sides.
- Push your nose forward and feel where your body tilts.
- Do the same with your head turned to the right.
- *Then to the left*
- Now gently pull your nose and head back and lean until you stop on your heels

Do you notice when you push your nose forward you automatically step forward. This is momentum and what it feels like to move forward.

When you push your nose out to the right or left, you simply lean to the side and stop. This is what it feels like to be in the present

When you pull your nose and head back, you stop at your heels and you can't fall backwards unless you force it. Forcing it is what it feels like to fall back into the past. However, stopping at the heels is reassurance that there is no going back.

Focus on Peace and Ease

Set a goal of peace and ease as you embrace change. It may not always be easy. There will be road blocks. But you'll be able to handle them with the **power** of love, joy, and forgiveness, instead of **forcing** change from fear, guilt and emotional pain. Similar to restoring your home, forcing the renovations for a quick result in your emotional life only leads to chaos later. It must be rebuilt with patience and consistency layer by layer. Once you embrace change and finish your own restoration, then you can experience the joy fully and invite others in to share it with you.

We, like the weather, have our cycles of change. Each storm, sunny day, and dark night all exist in a perfect synergy whether you are lying dormant or growing.

Chapter 8:
Joy is Possible

Joy is a net of love by which you can catch souls.
~ Mother Teresa

Being named Joy has truly been a blessing. It's common for people to tell me how they love that name. In my work with chronically ill and dying people, and their families, I was often the first person they met with to discuss one of the hardest decisions of their lives. In that time, they needed some joy in their life to balance out the grief and pain. At Southern Baptist church camp at Falls Creek, Oklahoma, we learned that JOY is an acronym:

Jesus, Others, You
In that order.

In reality, joy is not a top down hierarchy. This is not a "diss" against Jesus. He epitomized love and joy, and his message is still as strong as ever.

Joy, Others, You

Simultaneously intermingle with each other to create a beautiful synergy of giving, receiving, and the peace that joy brings. Joy shines on you and others so you can feel unconditional love and see new ways to interact together and help each other.

If you ask anyone on the street what they want in life, most people say they want more money and to be happy. But what does happy really mean? And how does it compare to joy? According to Transcending the Levels of Consciousness by David Hawkins:

> *"As Love becomes increasingly unconditional, it begins to be experienced as inner joy. This is not the sudden joy of a pleasurable turn of events, but instead a constant accompaniment to all activities. Joy arises from within each moment of existence rather from any outer source."*

This is how helping others and yourself compassionately steps in. The Dalai Lama shares, "If you want others to be happy, practice compassion. If you want to be happy, practice compassion." When you share your heart compassionately when someone is suffering, your presence softens their experience of being stuck in the lower level emotions. Being compassionate opens you up to freely share unconditional love without judgment, which leads to a state of joy in you and others. Notice how joy just happens. After loosening the chains of grief, it's just an ever-present way of life, like breathing.

The root word passion in compassion means suffering. But, real passion is associated with something that lights a fire of emotion in you while you're suffering to do what brings you joy! It's the fuel that drives you to your wildest dreams. What's your passion? Are you ready to pursue it? You've already suffered, but what's your trajectory now based on what your grief and loss have taught you?

My friend Jamie Lee Silver, has been through hell and back in the past 3 years. Her son Benjamin Lee was a champion cross country runner who received a full scholarship to Miami University in Ohio. He was a poet, a singer and songwriter who had a smile that made you feel both welcome and safe. Then he hit a rough patch. He injured his ankle and was unable to run with the team in college.

Jamie's dear son went from a bright beam of light to an extremely depressed person who didn't resemble himself at all. The grief of losing his passion caused him to spiral into an emotional chasm of despair. He lost his scholarship and spent the next two years in and out of hospitals as a terrible mental illness took over his brain. Jamie and her family tried desperately to help him.

Ben lost all of his hope and joy, and he eventually took his own life. I cannot imagine the horror of going through this with a child. The toll Ben's suicide took on his family and community was an intense reality check to be gracious about life.

Of course, Jamie and her family experienced deep levels of grieving and emptiness vacillating in between everyday life and work obligations with a huge boulder of emotions weighing them down. Also, I could not wrap my head or heart around my own grief around this beautiful person I saw grow up.

Nevertheless, in true Ben form, before his Celebration of Life, Ben came to me in a vision from the Other Side. Being the poet that he was, he channeled a poem through me to read at the celebration. It was about how he felt lost in a deep canyon of sorrow and couldn't get out. Then, while running joyously in Heaven, he explained how he is happier than ever now that his soul is free.

During his Mom's intuitive healing sessions with me, Ben came through and gave Jamie sage wisdom and advice about how to heal and what was in store for her future. Almost every time he appeared he was running toward her smiling a smile that can only exist in Heaven.

One of the key things he spoke about to Jamie was that he will speak with her through writing. Jamie, also a poet and avid writer, started journaling questions and messages for Ben, and then he would answer back to her. Eventually, she published a book of their Mom and Son love story together in *My Forever Ben, One Mom's Letters to her Son-in-spirit and his Poetic Replies*. Ben encouraged Jamie to find a new life and gave her the courage to move to the ocean in Florida to heal and live her own life.

Jamie, through Ben's messages, has since told her story through suicide prevention organizations such as Hope for the Day and others in Chicago and Florida. She's now an advocate for people going through loss, and is teaching Grief Relief/Wisdom Writing workshops using all the tools she has used to bring herself from a state of utter despair to a life where she is truly thriving and happy.

Every time she writes to Ben he has so much to tell her. He is her biggest cheerleader and constantly assures her they will be always together — their love is eternal. Jamie's greatest thrill is helping grieving people experience their own continuing connection with their loved-ones-in-spirit through their own pen. She teaches Wisdom Writing in workshops around Florida as well as helping people heal online. The Ben/Jamie team is flourishing as they, together, use their collective gifts to bring peace and hope to people dealing with suicide and other types of grief.

This is a beautiful example of how Joy is absolutely possible after grief and loss, or any stressful experiences, big or small, in your life.

Now that you're on the verge of change and identifying what your new journey has in store, it's important to acknowledge how you feel love and how you feel loved by others.

Exercise 1

Love Languages

The 5 Love Languages by Gary Chapman
- Gift giving
- Quality time
- Words of affirmation
- Acts of service (devotion)
- Physical touch

This is a way to identify what attributes make you or another person feel loved.
- What are your top 2 Love Languages?
- What are the top 2 Love Languages of your spouse, family members, friends or coworkers?

Tell the people which ones are important for you, and specifically, how they make you feel.

For others, demonstrate acts related to their love languages. Over time, notice if they become happier or more content around you. How do you feel when others express your love language?

This is the beginning of sharing and receiving love with your heart instead of your head, and releasing suffering so that unconditional love, gratitude, and forgiveness come to the surface every day.

Sharing love is crucial to staying in balance and keeping your joy tank full. In The HeartMath Solution by Doc Childre and Howard Martin, they write about how putting your physical heart out to the world has a measurable energy field. If you "put out your heart" to others, gratitude, compassion and love surround them, which creates you and the people around you to be more calm and coherent physically and emotionally. In the section on "Powering up Your Life," the authors write:

If you apply your heart first, your head can get in sync with your heart intelligence. By using your heart as your compass, you can see more clearly which direction to go to stop self-defeating behavior. Take one thing that really drains you and apply heart intelligence to it, you'll see a noticeable difference in your lif.... Creating a joint venture between your head and heart puts a power pack behind your goals. The head can notice what needs to change, but the heart provides the power and direction to bring about the change.

Applying Heart Intelligence

Applying heart intelligence is similar to telepathy from the brain. Instead of sending a thought out to another person, you put gratitude and love out from your heart area. In a HeartMath seminar I attended, the facilitator said to do the following:

- Envision a door in your heart area in the middle of your chest.
- Open that door wide and with every breath out, send out gratitude and love. I equate this to blowing up a balloon one breath at a time.
- This creates a "bubble of love" that extends out to the people, pets and plants in your proximity.

For more information on the transformative power of your heart intelligence, check out heartmath.org.

Who would have guessed that reversing negativity and sharing love could be so easy? It's automatic once you've cleared out the negativity, resistance, and emotional pain with some of the strategies mentioned in this book. Happiness and joy are still present even in a heavy emotional state. It's just not as big and open. The chart below illustrates that happiness is present no matter what you're feeling.

Happiness is ever present behind the clouds of your grief and loss. Joy has no clouds, only the sun shining in a clear sky. Knowing that you can put your heart out and create a beautiful synergy of love and joy for others and yourself, doesn't this inspire you to stay in this State of Being? To live lighter?

Joy is always possible. Joy is ever present. Getting to know your joy is a beautiful gift and invokes a promising today and tomorrow. Your joy is restored!

There are so many people who are starting campaigns for random or deliberate acts of kindness. My 8-year-old daughter Summer and I are starting a "Joy is Possible" campaign to spread love and light to anyone and everyone. We're starting by passing out sunshine yellow cards that say "Joy Is Always Possible" and thereby opening up connections with others. But ultimately, we have set an intention that whoever sees or receives the "Joy Is Always Possible" message will reawaken to what their life really means and that they have a reason for being in this world. More to come.

How Can You Spread Joy?
- Wear a bright colored scarf, shirt or other clothing on a cloudy day or any day, or when you'll be around people who are depressed or ill.
- Smile or laugh!! Whether you're in the grocery store, the bank or anywhere, smiling is infectious. Your smile could re-enliven the day for someone.
- Wave to strangers and friends. It creates a heart jump that we are acknowledged.
- Give someone a hug heart to heart and hang on a few seconds

longer than normal.
- Share your spiritual gifts.

Once your joy becomes a way of Being for you, your future can look brighter and your road opens up to possibilities, imagined and unimagined. Even when chaos, stress and grief enters in, it will be effortless for you to embrace that joy is possible.

Chapter 9:

O – The Open Road
Anything is Possible

Action changes you.
~ Robin Sharma, Author

In *The Power of Touch,* Phyllis Davis discusses a concept called skin hunger, which is a person's intense hunger to be touched. When I worked in nursing facilities, every resident was clinically touched by the nurses or nurse's aides to provide medical treatments and care such as bathing. But, these residents hungered for touch and connection that was not "work" related.

In the same way, people long for experiences once they're ready and willing to change. They have this innate need to ride forward to their new horizon, instead of just looking at it from afar. Realizing that your dreams can be real for you is so exciting! Whatever you hunger for awaits!

If you're offered a seat on a rocket ship, you don't ask
what seat. You just get on.
~ Sheryl Sandberg

Driving on the Open Road
Sometime in April around my birthday in 2004, I was living in Sacramento and had a job I loved. Life was pretty good too. But then I had a dream that shook me up. Usually my dreams were forgotten once I woke up, but this day I remember the clarity of a peace sign,

heart, yellow happy face, and a yin yang symbol. Then I saw a sign for Prescott and a road going there. I woke up and wondered where Prescott was and when I could go there.

Turns out it's a mountain town in Northern Arizona that I hadn't heard of before. When I looked it up online, my heart skipped a beat, like the feeling when you meet the person you're going to marry. My eyes welled up with tears because I knew from that moment on I had choice, but I was definitely being pulled to the mystery town. Peace, love, joy and balance were a part of that somehow. These symbols were the epitome of my core being, and gave substance to who I wanted to be and how I longed to live.

About one week later, I went into my boss's office gave her my six week notice. I told her I needed two days off to go to Prescott to find an apartment, so I could move there in June. I knew no one there and I had never been there before, but somehow I knew that place.

A few weeks later, I flew into Phoenix and drove a tiny Toyota rental car to the 5000 foot elevation. The feeling of being home and the beauty of the arid mountains filled me up with a light. A soft white light in my belly glowed peacefully. I thought, *I am doing this!*

Then, I drove through a town called Prescott Valley, a mecca of strip malls and a busy highway. Ugly. Disheartening. That's when I started to panic. *What am I doing?!?!* My breathing quickened, but I forged ahead.

Once Prescott Valley was in the rear view mirror, I found myself winding up a road where houses were above me on sides of mountains and cliffs. The trees turned from deciduous to conifer around each bend. I reached a peak, and looked down into the beautiful saloon infested, historical, mountain town of Prescott with the silhouette of Thumb Butte rising above the horizon.

The sigh I expelled could be heard around the town and I started crying a little bit. Relief was in those tears, but so was the feeling of being home. I parked and walked around the square. I sat with strangers and asked about the town. People looked happy there.

The next day I found an apartment next to the senior community built in the 1800's. I found out my neighbor was an artist named Jacques.

My friend Julie and I drove a U-Haul from Northern California to Arizona. I had left behind a job I loved, a boyfriend with a ton of potential for a long-term relationship, and many friends. But in Prescott, I found myself, both the neurotic Joy and the finally peaceful Joy.

Two weeks after I moved there, a guy named Joe came to my door. He said he's looking for a hospice patient, but he obviously had the wrong address. I told Joe that I loved hospice and would love to work there if anything opened up. A month later, I got a job with Kay and Bill at Preferred Home Care. Joe, it turns out, was a friend of theirs from Albuquerque.

About 7 months later, I had to get a job in Phoenix to pay my bills. It was heartbreaking to only be in Prescott for the weekends. But at day 90 of the Phoenix job, I gave my notice effective immediately because I had a feeling to get back to Prescott ASAP. I didn't know how I was going to make it financially, but I listened to my gut and a psychic friend who said to go back up the hill.

When I got back from a hike to Sedona, I looked in the want ads, and there was a job opening at Hospice Family Care for a marketing position. I applied, got the job, and was thrilled about the pay as well as the fact that I could work with seniors and caregivers again. Joe had been promoted to another branch. He trained me to take over his job, which changed the whole meaning of my purpose in life.

A year a half later, I met my husband, John, in downtown Prescott on a street corner. He asked me for directions, and 7 months later I was living with him in Illinois. Before I left, one of the last hospice patients I helped just happened to be from Lisle, Illinois, which is my husband's home town.

I had a lot of naysayers from family and friends about this literal and physical journey. If they didn't think I was crazy, they projected their fear of the unknown onto me. I had many doubts, worries and regrets in my freak out moments. It wasn't all butterflies and rainbows. However, I fully trusted the signs, my gut feeling, and just went there. I didn't let my thoughts impede taking this risk. I forged ahead with courage.

As a result, I discovered so many parts of myself that were buried under mistakes and regrets. Nevertheless, I could shine again and literally look out to the horizon from the highest peak.

Sometimes you have to get on the road, the boat, the airplane, or read that life changing book to go see what else is possible beyond your wildest dreams and imagination. Trust, faith and courage become your best friend. Grace steps in to guide you to peace after turmoil. What's possible may push you to embrace new ideas — see ways of being that were unseen in your life before. And often in these new beginnings (aka risks), there are big and small joys along the way that cancel out most of the hard stuff in the end.

> *I do not at all understand the mystery of grace - only that it meets us where we are, but does not leave us where it found us.*
> ~ Anne Lamott, Author

Grace
Kimberly Mills, God Seeker, Social Worker, and Bright Soul, has a beautiful take on Grace. She describes it as a clock face. Midnight is where the hardships and turmoil lie. As you move to the three, there is remorse. Moving onto the six opens up the opportunity to surrender, repent the past, and ask for forgiveness. At this point some people recoil back to remorse or to turmoil, but they can come back around to forgiveness.

The nine is pure, sweet Grace. The road to Grace can be bumpy, but once you arrive, the road is smooth and easy. There's a beautiful rest stop there waiting there just for you. At times, you may revert back to an emotional state where you have to surrender and forgive again, but that's ok. The important part is that once you reach Grace, very seldom will you experience that same emotional turmoil at midnight ever again.

So go forth, dear one. Ride that road and move ahead. Joy is on the horizon, but also your traveling companion. If it's a choice that's not in your highest good, then grace gives you a do over. The important thing is to keep the momentum going, even when you have to switch directions.

Exercise 1

Creating Your Virtual Road (Life) Trip

Write a navigation list of the roads you will take to get to joy.
- How will you get there?
- Where will you stay until you arrive?
- Who will you meet along the way?
- When will you need to fill up your tank again?

When you ride the open road and there are no barriers in your way, put on your cruise control, let the wind blow through your hair, and relish in having let go. You are free!

Chapter 10
You've Got This!

"So far you've survived 100% of your worst days.
And experienced 100% of your best ones."
~Unknown

One night I had a vivid dream that Tony Robbins and I were traveling together. He was with me in the airport. I had to apologize to him because turns out we didn't need to wait in the long line to go through baggage claim. Then I noticed he was looking at what was in my bag. There was a piece of dog poop in a cardboard hot dog holder and the donkey from the movie *Shrek*. I told Tony that at times I'm full of shit and sometimes I'm an ass, but most of the time I'm inspiring.

Then he asked me, "Where do we go next, Joy? I can tell you the right way, but you can follow your own heart and then we will travel ahead." I laughed joyously and closed my eyes while holding excited fists at my hips and told him, "I do know the way. I'll tap into it now!"

Then I woke up and felt exhilarated! First of all, the people we see in our dreams represent a part of ourselves. Second, the dream meaning of busy airports signifies the desire for freedom, high ideals, ambition, and hopes. It also indicates that you are ready to take off with a new idea and you may be experiencing a new career path or adventure. Most importantly it illustrated how ready I am to restore my own joy and help you restore yours.

Arrivals and departures fill our days. Babies are born, we see long lost friends, new opportunities arise.

Then, the departures of loved ones who have passed, jobs lost, relationships ended, and the old you.

The true you is here now, a bright shining star that has shown up to face life no matter what it brings. Every moment is a new start, a new arrival. Smile, dear one. There is nothing holding you back from joy now. Step out the door and be fully you.

You have arrived at your destination! Now that you know you've made this happen, what's next?

Epilogue

I have to admit, while I was writing this book, I was faced with a considerable number of stressors, states of emotions, and learning curves. However, as I reviewed what I had written throughout the editing process, I invariably saw a quote, a strategy, or a reminder that I could apply to myself and my situation at that moment as a human — not as the author.

Today in particular, I'm feeling out of sorts, partially due to a virus, partially due to personal fears and taking on too much of other people's stuff. The immune system waxes and wanes in response to states of being and states of emotions respectively.

The phrase "shift your attention" from Gary Zukav helped me today. Yesterday, it was about letting go of the rope of control and resistance.

I believe you too will find the right passage at the right time to use any day or anytime you struggle, feel lost or alone, or just need some encouragement. At least, that's the intention I set for all of you who resonate with this travelogue through grief.

Besides, we humans are all traveling on the same grief road to joy. Some of us are speeding by on the shoulder. Some are frustrated sitting in traffic, while others are coasting along with a smile on their face listening to some tunes. Some are walking instead of waiting for the cars to move. Getting to your destination is easier with continuous momentum. But, some have pulled off to the shoulder to take a break and reset. Some are helping others with a flat tire or with jumper cables. But we are all, nevertheless, moving forward.

Each moment is a step closer to the destination. Maybe you see joy on the horizon. Or, maybe you've already arrived. But, for all of you, congratulations for living each day a bit better.

Similar to prisoners keeping tally marks of the days in their jail cells, we can keep a measure to see how far we've come since our losses. It might be journaling, going to see a psychologist, intuitive healer, or energy worker, or gradually feeling less heavy about anything reminding you about your losses.

It's all in the willingness to live, forgive, and see the potential of what else is possible.

And so, here we go again on your own and together.

Peace and Love,
Joy Lucinda

Bibliography

Satir, Virginia, *The Satir Model: Family Therapy and Beyond*, Science and Behavior Books, 1991.

Davis, Phyllis, *The Power of Touch: The Basis for Survival, Health, Intimacy and Emotional Well-Being* by Phyllis Davis, Hay House, 1999.

Smith, Linda, *Healing Oils, Healing Hands (2nd Edition)*, HTSM Publishing, 2008.

Childre, Doc and Martin, Howard, *The HeartMath Solution: The Institute of HeartMath's Revolutionary Program for Engaging the Power of the Heart's Intelligence*, HarperOne, 2011.

Luthans, Fred, et al, re: *Psychological Capital*, http://www.annual-reviews.org/doi/full/10.1146/annurev-orgpsych-032516-113324

Orloff, M.D., Judith, *Positive Energy: 10 Extraordinary Prescriptions for Transforming Fatigue, Stress, and Fear into Vibrance, Strength, and Love*, Three Rivers Press, 2004.

Recommended Books
and Websites

You Can Heal Your Life by Louise Hay

Your Body's Telling You: Love Yourself! by Lisa Barbeau

Energy Medicine: Balancing Your Body's Energies for Optimal Health, Joy and Vitality by Donna Eden and David Feinstein

What to Say When You Talk To Yourself by Shem Helmstetter

The Four Agreements by Don Miguel Ruiz

Change Your Words, Change Your Life by Wayne Dyer

The Untethered Soul by Michael Singer

My Forever Ben, One Mom's Letters to her Son-in-spirit and his Poetic Replies by Jamie Lee Silver (On Amazon)

Healing With Nature by Susan S. Scott

Dakota by Kathleen Norris

The Power of Now by Eckhart Tolle

Healing After Loss: Daily Meditations for Working Through Grief by Martha Whitmore Hickman

Harlene's Bears to Cherish https://www.facebook.com/bearsto-cherish/about

What's Your Grief www.whatsyourgrief.com

Made in the USA
Columbia, SC
10 December 2018